D0016184

Anatomy of
a Kidnapping

Anatomy of
a Kidnapping

A Doctor's
Story

Steven L. Berk, M.D.

Texas Tech University Press

Copyright © 2011 by Steven L. Berk
Photographs copyright © 2011 by Phillip Periman

All rights reserved. No portion of this book may be reproduced in any
form or by any means, including electronic storage and retrieval systems,
except by explicit prior written permission of the publisher. Brief passages
excerpted for review and critical purposes are excepted.

This book is typeset in Scala. The paper used in this book meets the minimum requirements of ANSI/NISO Z39.48-1992 (R1997). ∞

Photography by Phillip Periman

Designed by Kasey McBeath

Library of Congress Cataloging-in-Publication Data
Berk, S. L. (Steven L.), 1949–
    Anatomy of a kidnapping : a doctor's story / Steven L. Berk.
       p. cm.
    Summary: "Tells the story of Steven L. Berk, M.D., who was kidnapped
from his home in Amarillo, Texas, in March of 2005. Shows how Berk
used his experiences and training as a physician to survive the ordeal and
bring his captor to justice"—Provided by publisher.
    ISBN 978-0-89672-693-2 (hbk. : alk. paper) 1. Berk, S. L. (Steven L.), 1949–
—Kidnapping, 2005. 2. Kidnapping victims—Texas—Case studies. 3.
Kidnapping—Texas—Case studies. I. Title.
    HV6574.U6B47 2011
    364.15'4092—dc22   2011015650

Printed in the United States of America
11 12 13 14 15 16 17 18 19 / 9 8 7 6 5 4 3 2

Texas Tech University Press
Box 41037 | Lubbock, Texas 79409-1037 USA
800.832.4042 | ttup@ttu.edu | www.ttupress.org

To the many crime victims whose stories have not been heard

I love those who can smile in trouble, who can gather strength from distress, and grow brave by reflection.

Leonardo da Vinci

Contents

CONTENTS

Illustrations

Acknowledgments

Julia Weiser, a Yale graduate and first-year medical student at the University of Texas Southwestern, edited this book. Julia understood what I wanted to convey in my story, especially as it relates to physicians and young doctors. Her detailed questions to me about my kidnapping and experiences in medicine helped improve the message. She also encouraged me to include some of the more personal insights about family and patients.

To my family—Jeremy, Justin, and Shirley—whose strength in facing the kidnapping made the book a more compelling commitment.

Thanks to the city of Amarillo and the West Texas community, especially the Amarillo police force, the district attorney's office, and the *Amarillo Globe-News*.

To Leslie: you were an important reason for writing this book.

Thank you to the special lady who stopped her car on that Bushland road and let me use her cell phone.

ACKNOWLEDGMENTS

Barry Peterson and his staff helped me find legal references.

Dr. Abraham Verghese and Dr. Anand Karnad, former students, chief residents, and physician authors, provided important reviews of the book.

Many colleagues read the book and made suggestions: Dr. Rick Jordan, Dr. Steve Urban, Dr. Marjorie Jenkins, Dr. Thomas McGovern, Dr. Afzal Siddiqui, and Dr. John Baldwin. Dr. Robert Kimbrough MACP, a member of the American Osler Society and national expert on the life of William Osler, died in Lubbock, Texas, on November 24, 2010. His counsel on the life of Osler was inspiring to me and all his colleagues.

To my mom, age eighty-eight, who so wanted the book to be published during her lifetime. She helped me keep its completion a priority. And to my dad—I still miss him every day.

In addition to being an excellent physician and oncologist, Phillip Periman is an outstanding professional photographer and provided photographs of the kidnapping trail.

Dr. Robert Mandel taught me about the perplexing publishing business.

To the many colleagues—too many to name individually—who made my career and the experiences in Boston, Tennessee, and at Texas Tech University worth writing about.

I have changed the names of my patients and in certain instances changed some of the details of the cases to further protect their identity.

Prologue

did not know the difference between a rifle and a shotgun, but I knew that the black metal barrel aimed at my forehead by this agitated stranger had the potential to blast my carefully constructed life into fragments.

There is no prescription or special behavior appropriate for the victim of violent crime, but as a doctor I reflect on the moment with some special understanding. Violence, trauma, rehabilitation, sorrow, and death have a special significance in the life and career of a physician, for they accompany the patients whom one has taken an oath to serve.

I am not the usual crime victim. And I quickly saw my captor as no ordinary criminal. I saw his struggle through the eyes of a doctor. If he was addicted to drugs, I had treated the drug addict. If he was a victim of abuse as a child, I had intervened in such abuse. If he was psychotic or sociopathic, such behavior I understood as part of a disease process.

Unfortunately, I had learned the consequences of trauma and violence from a big-city emergency room: shattered skulls, indescribable facial disfigurations, rapid exsanguinations, gaping chest wounds, shocked and desperate family members. Fortunately, however, I had also learned "aequanimitas," the ability to stay calm and rational at all times.

It is a beautiful day in early March. Sunshine falls on quiet backyards and alleys in Amarillo, the only sounds a chorus of barking dogs, the cackle of blackbirds, and the tinkle of wind chimes. An intermittent melody is heard from my son's guitar as he practices in our basement. My wife, Shirley, has left for church. Jeremy, away at college, has sent me an e-mail and is awaiting my input on a research paper.

Dressed in pressed khaki pants and a Stanford T-shirt, Justin comes up from the game room to the main floor of our home. He wants to say a quick good-bye before being picked up by a friend to go to church. Heading for the front door, he turns and sees me for an instant as I lean my head from the laundry room into the hallway. We exchange good-byes. He does not know why I am in the laundry room on that Sunday morning, and could never imagine that my life is being threatened by a criminal who has quietly entered our home. As Justin leaves, I realize I may be seeing him for the last time, and yet I am robbed of the opportunity to speak from the heart to my teenage son who might end the day without a father. This is only the beginning of a day that will require all I have learned as a physician, counselor, healer, and thinker to survive.

For several years I have reflected on my kidnapping and the insights it has given me about life and death, crime, the practice of medicine, and the physician-patient relationship. I write this book to share these reflections with the students and residents who are training to become physicians, with other crime victims for whom I have a special understanding, and with those in West Texas who remember my story and find inspiration in its outcome.

Anatomy of
a Kidnapping

The Doctor

Keams Canyon is an ancient sandstone valley in north-eastern Arizona, a vast expanse of open sky, pine tree-topped cliffs, and countless layers of brown earth. At sunset, the towering walls of the canyon turn unimaginable shades of orange and red. In the midst of this awesome setting sits Keams Canyon Indian Hospital, a small, two-story building located near the end of the winding dirt road that constitutes Main Street for this zip code in Arizona. The hospital is located on the Hopi Indian Reservation in Navajo County, and it serves two of the most culturally intact Indian tribes in the continental United States. Thousands of square miles dotted by small mud huts called hogans make up the enormous geographic expanse that relies on this single facility for medical care.

In 1975, I spent four months working in the isolated hospital at Keams, from March through June. I was a young, idealistic, fourth-year medical student from Boston University, looking for hands-on medical training and experience working with patients from a completely different cultural background. I was born in New York, raised in New Jersey, and educated in Massachusetts. I wanted my experience in Keams to quite literally broaden my horizons.

I was not disappointed. The tiny hospital had fewer than forty beds and served a population of over fifteen thousand. It was understocked and understaffed, and even as a medical student I was often expected to do the work of a full-fledged physician. Within weeks, I was seeing and treating patients on my own. Finally, I had the opportunity to put everything I had learned from lectures and textbooks into real practice. I was learning something new every single day, and enjoying every moment of it.

It was May, and the temperatures had been steadily rising as the summer heat began to settle over the canyon. The hospital was air-conditioned and my small apartment was not, so I was glad to spend the entire day at work. I was staffing the clinic on the first floor of the hospital when a three-year-old Navajo boy was brought in by his worried mother. The woman told me his symptoms: fever and sore throat. These are typical complaints for a toddler, and especially common in children from Native American populations, which are genetically more susceptible to many infectious diseases.

The child did not speak, did not cry, but stared wide-eyed at the non-Native American doctor who told him to open his mouth and say "Ahh." I knew from my coursework and from experience on the reservation that this was probably just an infection of streptococcal bacteria: strep throat. The symptoms are fever and throat pain, and on examination the throat will look red and inflamed. If the patient does not have a runny nose or a cough— suggesting a viral infection—the diagnosis of strep can be confirmed by throat culture, and treatment can be prescribed immediately. Strep was one of the most common problems we saw at Keams, and it was usually easy to diagnose and treat with antibiotics.

However, upon examination, this boy's throat looked unusual. I saw the typical redness that accompanies sore throat, but I also noticed a thin, ominous, gray membrane extending over the back of his throat to his uvula (the protuberance that dangles from the palette at the back of the mouth). The lymph nodes in the child's neck were enlarged. His heart sounds were distant, and I had trouble hearing them when I pressed my stethoscope to his chest. The clues were adding up, and I recognized this disease, not from real-life experience, but from my battered copy of *Harrison's Principles of Internal Medicine*. I remembered the biology of disease course and pictured my class notes, trying to visualize the photograph in *Harrison's* and remember the slide from the infectious diseases lectures. Yes, it was coming together, and I realized that this patient was not suffering from strep throat.

An experienced internal medicine professor would often say, "When you hear hoofbeats, think horses, not zebras." He was emphasizing that the simplest explanation for a piece of evidence is usually the right explanation. But this time I knew a zebra was galloping across Keams Canyon. The Navajo boy had common symptoms, but they were the result of an uncommon problem. His sore throat and fever were not signs of strep, but symptoms of the rare and dangerous disease called diphtheria. Diphtheria! As I considered the unusual diagnosis, my heart began to race, and I flushed at the thought of making this important discovery on my own. Just three months before, I was still a bumbling medical student, but now I was on the verge of making an important diagnosis that had major implications for the hospital and the community.

Diphtheria is uncommon in the United States but has been

reported among the Navajo. It is a potentially deadly problem and can cause epidemics that are particularly dangerous to children. The last major outbreak in the United States was in New England in the 1700s, but more recently, in 1943, a diphtheria epidemic in Europe killed over fifty thousand people. The disease has become rare because of a successful vaccine, but it is still extremely dangerous. Not all children are immunized, and even with antibiotics, about 20 percent of children who become infected will die.

After examining the boy, I ordered a throat culture to confirm my diagnosis. But I knew how quickly the disease could spread to others, and I did not want to wait a week for the results. I began treatment for diphtheria immediately and called for public health assistance. That very day, a nurse went throughout the reservation, from hogan to hogan, conducting a surveillance study to identify and treat other potential cases of the disease.

A week later, I got a call from the microbiology lab on the first floor of the hospital: "Throat culture—child named Begay, Edward Begay—positive for *Corynebacterium diphtheriae*." Another child from a nearby hogan, part of the surveillance study, was also positive for the disease. More cases were confirmed in the next few days, but because we had worked quickly and caught the outbreak early, not a single child died from diphtheria in that summer of 1975.

My successful diagnosis of diphtheria and active participation in preventing an epidemic was the culmination of a long series of experiences that had transformed me from an inexperienced medical student into a competent physician. During my months at Keams, I gained experience in every aspect of patient care and learned the basic skills that make up the fundamentals of practicing medicine. Every week, there was a new lesson, and a new role for me to fill.

At Keams, I was not just a medical student, I was a radiologist. A Navajo man came in complaining of persistent chest pain. He had been injured while chopping wood several weeks before, and while the skin had healed where shards of ax had entered his chest, he still suffered from sharp pains whenever he breathed. I performed an X-ray and found the sliver of metal that was still embedded deep in his chest. It had penetrated his chest wall, but thankfully it had not yet pierced his heart or lungs. I ordered a surgery to remove the ax shard, and the patient recovered without complications.

I was an obstetrician. A young woman arrived at clinic in the middle of labor, worried that she was going to die during her first pregnancy. I examined her and found that she was in the later stages of delivery, but that she and the baby were both in good condition. I calmly reassured the mother that everything was going to be okay. Just an hour later, she delivered a healthy baby boy without complications.

I was a pharmacist. A child came down with a bothersome inner ear infection, and her mother brought her in for treatment. It was a typical infection, and I prescribed a round of antibiotics. The girl was too young to swallow pills, so I prepared the medicine myself, using a mortar and pestle to create a syrup of liquid ampicillin, fruit flavored so that the child would be more likely to finish the entire course of treatment.

I was a neurologist. I was the person on call when a local shaman came to the hospital complaining of an abrupt change in his personality. He was an important member of his tribe, and his family and neighbors were worried by his recent agitation and strange behavior. I suspected he was suffering from advanced syphilis, a bacterial infection that can remain dormant for years before manifesting itself through severe neurological complications. At that stage of the disease, the only way to confirm a diagnosis is to check the patient's spinal fluid for infection. I had to perform a spinal tap, a fairly common but sometimes difficult procedure. After injecting a local anesthesia into the patient's back, I inserted a long, thin needle into the spinal column between his fourth and fifth vertebrae. I drew out the spinal fluid and sent it to the lab for analysis. They confirmed the diagnosis of syphilis, and the shaman responded to an aggressive treatment of penicillin, which prevented the further deterioration of his brain and other vital organs.

Performing a spinal tap is something that almost every medical student is called upon to do in his or her fourth year. Because it is a high-pressure procedure, performing your first lumbar puncture is a rite of passage that many students remember for the rest of their careers. I was proud that I had done mine without complications. The medical milestones I reached at Keams—delivering a baby, performing a lumbar puncture, successfully reading an X-ray—were all important steps in building my confidence and competence as a physician. Because Keams was so understaffed, it felt to me like I was on the fast track of medical training, but in fact these were skills I would have learned in any hospital in the country. However, I learned other lessons at Keams that I could not have learned at most other hospitals. I had chosen Keams as the site of my fourth-year training because I knew that in the end it would offer me more than just competence.

At Keams, I treated patients whose cultural and religious backgrounds were completely different from my own. I gained intimate knowledge of Native American culture and witnessed firsthand how differences in backgrounds, beliefs, and traditions influence patient care. Through my experience with patients who spoke a different language and interpreted the world in a completely different way, I learned that the practice of medicine does not just involve making the right diagnosis or prescribing the right medicine. Above all, it involves listening carefully to patients and understanding where they are coming from. I learned that mutual respect and understanding are a fundamental part of patient care.

This lesson was driven home during my first month at Keams, when a clash of cultures thundered through the quiet valley. The tribal council, a group of elected leaders from both the Hopi and Navajo tribes, had been called to address a volatile issue that had come up between the physicians and patients at Keams Canyon Indian Hospital. Navajo and Hopi elders, young Caucasian physicians, and nurses—many of them Native Americans—had gathered to address conflict and controversy.

The small clinic classroom was crowded and very warm, despite the cool breeze that swept across the canyon on that typical evening in spring. The participants stood around the edge of the room, leaning against the public health posters hanging on the walls, which listed the symptoms of tuberculosis and gonorrhea. They fidgeted and chose to ignore the empty foldout chairs that had been set out. Clearly, everyone was hoping that we would all be able to leave soon.

A Navajo elder—dark-skinned, somber, wearing a velveteen shirt with bolo tie—began the discussion, speaking slowly as though he regretted having to communicate by speech at all.

"My niece, a nurse here, has told me this," he said with passion and controlled anger. "Doctor put the tube, the breathing tube, down the throat after man is dead. And also he put needle in his chest after he is already dead." He pointed to a young physician standing near the door of the conference room. The room fell quiet. There was palpable tension, as if the doctor was on trial. As if we all were on trial.

Everyone's attention turned to the physician by the door, who stood tall, towering over the group in his jeans and T-shirt. He seemed confident and somewhat arrogant, anxious to make his case, to explain the obvious. He too spoke with controlled passion, pride, and indignation.

"This is routine," he told the elder matter-of-factly. "This is accepted practice. The tube, the endotracheal tube, is needed when someone stops breathing or sometimes when someone has a heart attack. Under those circumstances we need to be able to put it in quickly or the patient will die. To do that, we need to practice."

There was a gasp of disapproval at the term "practice." Some had not heard this before—that doctors would "practice" doing a procedure on dead patients.

"Not on the dead!" replied the elder.

The young physician continued with the same condescending tone, like a teacher patiently waiting for his pupil to understand. Perhaps he was thinking about the teaching hospital he had attended in Iowa where, after a patient died, his team would practice different procedures with the curtain drawn. They would perform an intubation on the deceased, forcing a tube down the trachea to open up the airway to the lungs. It is a difficult procedure to perform in an emergency, and a procedure that results in death if performed incorrectly. His team would also practice finding important veins or arteries in patients who had died in the hospital. They would use a needle to access the subclavian vein beneath the collarbone or the femoral artery in the groin. Knowing exactly where to find these points of access could mean the difference between life and death in an emergency, and the doctor from Iowa firmly believed in the need to "practice" these procedures in a controlled setting.

He replied to the Navajo elder, failing to keep the frustration out of his voice, "Of course we must practice on the dead. One cannot practice on the living."

The Navajo participants seemed to move toward each other as if there were two magnets in the room, separating one people from another. The Hopi nurses also stirred, instinctively drawing away from the white nurses and doctors as if they were trying to escape contamination. Though the Navajo and Hopi tribes have distinct histories, traditions, and cultures, that night they shared the same goal: there would be no practicing on the Native American dead. Both tribes agreed that there must be respect for the dead, that practicing intubation on a dead patient was taboo, unacceptable, American. The Hopi and Navajo have different beliefs about the afterlife, but they both agree that disturbing the body of a dead person also disturbs the soul of that person and disrupts an important journey from one level of existence to another.

"There should be no need to practice on the dead. Why can't doctors come here who already know what they are doing?" a young Navajo asked.

A Hopi nurse agreed. "Come here *after* you know what to do."

Another doctor answered defensively, "We come here without adequate support. There are no anesthesiologists available to do intubations here, no specialists of any kind. We need to be able to perform these procedures ourselves, and this is the only way for us to learn. If you want us to help the living, we need to practice on the dead. And not just intubation, but other procedures as well."

In some cases, biomedical practices and traditional beliefs can coexist: a Native American pneumonia patient would visit both a doctor and a tribal medicine man for treatment. However, the issue of training for emergency procedures on cadavers was different. The tribal elders and the nurses held firmly to their religious convictions, and the physicians should have recognized the futility of arguing further. No one spoke further for the Navajo or Hopi. The debate was over. There would be no practice on the dead, ever, under any circumstances. Several physicians disagreed, but the decision had been made. The young doctor from Iowa was clearly upset. For the rest of his time at Keams, I could tell that he was counting down the days until he could leave. He felt his learning experience had been undermined by cultural misunderstandings.

My medical education at Keams was illuminating. It taught me not only the skills I would need as a physician, but also the patience I would need to practice medicine in any context. I valued the experiences and interactions I had with people whose beliefs I did not share. They made me realize that helping people involves understanding them first, a lesson that has served me well over decades of practicing medicine.

I left Keams with a plan to return after completing my residency. After graduation, new physicians are required to enter training programs called residencies that prepare them for their chosen specialties. I would have gladly continued working at Keams, but they did not have a certified residency training program, and so I was set to return to Boston for the next four years of my career. I had known since March where I would be practicing, having received the important news over the phone just a week after I arrived in Arizona.

Medical schools in the United States have a very complicated system for placing graduating students in training residencies across the country. After an extensive interview process, residency programs and prospective residents each submit the rankings of their options to a central matching service called the National Resident Matching Program. The NRMP uses a computer algorithm to place each applicant, theoretically optimizing the matches based on the rankings. On "Match Day" every March, the NRMP releases the results of the match, and fourth-year students find out where they will be practicing the following July. Though graduation is still months away, Match Day is perhaps the most exciting and nerve-racking day of the year.

On March 20, 1975, I was far away from the excitement and pomp of Boston University's Match Day celebration. On that day all the graduating students gathered together to open their match letters at the same time. Having already settled into my small apartment in Keams, I could only imagine the tears and shouts of joy as 150 of my peers ripped open their envelopes and found out simultaneously where they would spend the most important years of their professional lives.

My girlfriend gave me the news over the phone: I had been matched at Boston City Hospital, my second choice. It was not unexpected and was more than acceptable. My original hopes for Massachusetts General Hospital had faded in November. During my interview there, I was given a theoretical scenario in which an intern reported certain heart sounds that led to a diagnosis. I accepted my hypothetical colleague's information, which turned out to be inaccurate. The point of the exercise was that I should have listened to the heart sounds myself instead of trusting the results of someone else's examination.

In retrospect, Boston City Hospital was the ideal training center for me. Massachusetts General Hospital was more prestigious and perhaps attracted more Harvard grads, but BCH would provide me with the best day-to-day, hands-on training that I could get. I admired the residents and faculty of BCH for their intense intellectual curiosity, and I appreciated the hospital's history, which was reflected in its classic teaching amphitheaters, its many medical wards, and its ancient laboratories. At Boston City, I would become part of a long tradition of excellence.

In July of 1975, just months after living with Native Americans on the vast plains of Arizona, I reported for duty at Boston City Hospital, which is nestled in the heart of inner-city Boston. I traded sunny days and cool nights, wide-open spaces, and mystical culture for a hot and muggy city hospital, which emanated the stench of urine, alcohol, and vomitus.

At that time, residents at BCH were assigned long shifts, regularly working thirty-six hours straight without seeing the light of day. We had come to BCH because we wanted to learn important skills and medical procedures, but also diligence, hard work, and patience; and so we obliged when they asked us to work more than a hundred hours per week. As residents, we were responsible for the scut work: drawing patients' blood, performing each routine lab test in the makeshift ward laboratories, and wheeling patients all over the hospital, from the emergency room to the wards. Somehow, we all survived through camaraderie, commitment, and countless pots of coffee.

I started out as the "night float," the intern who works the shift from 9:00 p.m. until around noon the next day. The rotation was established at BCH to improve working conditions in the 1930s, when residents were coming down with tuberculosis from lack of sleep, poor nutrition, and stress. The shift is lonelier and less supervised than other assignments, but it guarantees that other interns get a few hours of much-needed sleep. As a result, working as the night float is considered both a chore and a badge of honor.

Being the night float was a strange educational experience. At night, weird things happened in Boston City Hospital, and my memories from that time are a jumbled, almost dreamlike stream of sights, sounds, and smells.

I would come to the emergency room to evaluate a new patient. After the initial examination, I would wheel him back to the hospital ward on a stretcher loaded with an EKG monitor and whatever other equipment I needed packed in on the side or even on top of the patient. A long basement hallway connected the emergency room with the main hospital, and navigating the trip with a fully loaded stretcher was no easy task. I remember there was an inexplicable incline at the end of the hallway leading to the main elevators. An intern had to learn quickly exactly when to begin running in order to get the momentum to make it up that hill. In July, a new intern might be seen in backward motion, headed the wrong way down the incline with a frantic patient in tow.

That hallway was always full of strange sights. I remember its stark gray concrete floors and the faint smell of iodine from intravenous line dressings. Sometimes the iodine was overpowered by the stronger smell of urine—the result of a young man's seizure or an older man's incontinence. The hospital tunnels were also a frequent nighttime haunt for people who did not want to sleep on the streets. Many were just looking for shelter, but others would be passed out or quite sick (usually from alcohol), and an intern could put the sick individuals on a stretcher and wheel them to the inpatient ward to get credit for an admission.

Though my memories from being the night float (and especially of those dark and strangely populated basement hallways) often blur together, there are other events and individuals from my internship at Boston City Hospital that stand out with perfect clarity in my mind. I was constantly learning from my experiences during those three years, but some lessons were more memorable than others. Whether it was the death of a long-term patient, the mistake of a medical student under my supervision, or a single dramatic moment in the emergency room, these moments shaped—and continue to shape—the type of physician I am today.

When I first saw Mr. Hudson, he was in the emergency room having a seizure, his arms and legs flailing violently. A wide flat wooden stick protruded from his grimacing mouth, having been placed there by a nurse to prevent him from biting his own tongue.

Seizures have many causes, but at BCH in 1975, alcohol withdrawal was number one. If other potential causes—such as epilepsy or head trauma—were ruled out, patients might even be discharged on the same day to return to the street. That is what happened to Mr. Hudson, but unlike some patients who suffer from alcoholism, he returned to the hospital clinic for long-term follow-up and became a regular patient of mine.

Mr. Hudson had light brown skin, gray hair, and a big smile. His confident, booming voice suggested his background as a preacher, a career that he had sadly drowned in alcohol. For one year, I met him for his routine clinic visits. He would come in regularly for problems related to alcohol abuse. Drinking had damaged many of his vital organs. Alcoholic hepatitis caused severe episodes of pain in his liver as well as jaundice and fever. Alcoholic gastritis caused dangerous bleeding in his stomach. He was admitted for withdrawal seizures, mental health counseling, and consults with nutritionists to help bring his drinking problem under control and heal the damage he had done to his body.

Though Mr. Hudson was one of my most complicated cases, he was also one of my favorite patients, and over the course of our time together we had developed a relationship of mutual admiration and respect. Nearly twelve months after his initial seizure in the ER, Mr. Hudson was in good health under my care.

But I remember the day he came to clinic without the confidence and optimism that had sustained him during even the lowest moments of his battle with alcoholism. He entered the exam room looking serious and sullen, and he did not greet me with his usual jovial inquiry about how I was doing or about the well-being of his previous intern, Dr. Applegate. Usually he brought a piece of paper with a handwritten list of questions about his health, but today he had only one question for me.

"What's this knot?" he asked with concern. His usually strong pastor's voice sounded strained.

"Knot?"

"Lump," he said, looking straight at me. He wanted to get to the point.

I put pressure on the spot he indicated, palpating with the tips of my fingers above his clavicle. Sometimes the lymph nodes in the neck can become enlarged and tender when the body's immune system works overtime to fight off an infection. They will feel spongy and soft, like a stale marshmallow. But the mass over Mr. Hudson's collarbone was hard, more like a walnut. It was fixed to the underlying tissue and did not move as a lymph node would have.

I knew immediately what that knot meant, and I suspect that my patient did too.

"Is it cancer?"

Mr. Hudson was both knowledgeable and intuitive. And by that point in our relationship, he knew me. He knew that my usual positive spin on things would not work that day.

"I think it is. We'll have to find out."

A week after his appointment, a biopsy revealed that Mr. Hudson had a malignant lymphoma. We immediately began to fight the cancer just as we had the alcoholism. I told him that cancer is not always a fatal disease. Like his drinking problem, this was something we could overcome.

He asked, "Why me?" The alcohol-associated problems he could understand, but *Why cancer? Why now?*

I could have said, "Well, this cancer is associated with alcohol use. It's more likely to occur in the alcoholic." But I chose not to use this explanation. Instead, I told him what I have told patients throughout my career: there was no explanation. We cannot always understand why one person is afflicted with a certain disease and another is spared, why some live and others die.

Sometimes life does not provide us with an explanation for why things turn out the way they do. We cannot predict who will return from war, and who will never come home. We do not know why one person dies in a car accident and another person walks away whole. We cannot explain why someone dies the victim of a violent crime while someone else is spared. This same uncertainty about life and death pervades medicine, and so I did not have an explanation that would comfort Mr. Hudson when he asked me, "Why?"

As Mr. Hudson's treatment progressed, he continued to struggle with his unexpected diagnosis. Like many cancer patients, he was angry and heartbroken. He had worked so hard to overcome his alcoholism, and this new challenge was particularly devastating. However, just as he had faced his drinking problem, Mr. Hudson pursued his cancer treatment aggressively and courageously.

I recall looking for a vein on Mr. Hudson's gnarled, dark hands to start his chemotherapy. Many of his veins had been used up long ago, in numerous previous hospital admissions, and I had experience finding the few surviving vessels that could be used to deliver his medicine intravenously. In the months that he was getting chemo, I would sometimes visit his ward just to start his IVs. I was not always the physician on duty, but I was the only one who knew where his veins might be found. Once I found one on the top of his foot. Later, as his rounds of chemo wore on, he would trust only me to find that vein. For me, continuing to find and access that blood vessel was an important part of keeping up hope that Mr. Hudson would survive this cancer.

However, after several months of aggressive treatment, Mr. Hudson began to show the signs of a losing battle. The cancer had invaded his bone marrow, so his platelet count dropped and he began to develop bruises all over his body. His arms were covered in deep purple spots in the places we had drawn blood to conduct tests. A tumor in his chest was compressing his esophagus, and he had difficulty swallowing. As a result of this and a general loss of appetite, he suffered dramatic weight loss, and his face became gaunt and hollow. He experienced drenching sweats that soaked through his pajamas, a symptom that mocked our attempts to find an infectious cause. The cancer itself had inflamed his body's immune system to react in this way.

The most telling sign that Mr. Hudson was approaching the end was a change in the general expression of his face. Despite his suffering, his features eventually settled into a peaceful look. It is a look that I have seen several times as a physician, an expression that arrives quietly on the faces of dying patients, like a ship cruising gently into port after a storm. After months of disbelief, anger, and tears, Mr. Hudson finally achieved this look of peaceful acceptance. He died shortly after.

Mr. Hudson was the first patient I developed a close relationship with to die under my care. During the two years he spent as my patient, he must have noticed how frequently I searched my white coat pockets in vain for a pen to make progress notes. On the day before he died, he presented me with a gift. I was standing by his bed when he stretched out his hand and said simply, "I want you to have this pen, from me." I think the gesture was the only way he knew to say thank you.

It was a plastic ballpoint pen, pale green with a white tip. I have never used the same pen for more than a week—ever. But to this day, I keep Mr. Hudson's pen in a fancy box on my desk at home, a memento of death, suffering, and injustice, but also of nobility.

As a physician, I have proudly played a role in memorable medical victories; I have been a part of inspiring recoveries, joyful births, and miraculous cures. It is a privilege of my profession to play an active role in these types of moments, to fight and defeat suffering, disability, and disease. However, there are times when a physician is just another powerless witness to the forces of life and death. I could not explain to Mr. Hudson the injustice of his illness, and his pen serves as a reminder of the limits of my profession. However, it also reminds me of the courage and nobility Mr. Hudson displayed throughout his life and at his death. He fought and defeated alcoholism. He fought and succumbed to cancer. At every stage, Mr. Hudson inspired me with his strength of character and spirit, and his pen reminds me of these lessons.

Any hospital will provide a doctor with important lessons about the medical profession, but a teaching hospital is a particularly challenging and exciting place to teach and learn medicine. At

BCH, a diverse group of students and faculty came together from many different medical backgrounds. We all had our own ideas about best practices and patient care, and we were all trying to keep up with the latest facts and recommendations. Having medical students around always kept things exciting, since their freshness and inexperience was a constant source of lessons for all of us.

As a senior resident in my second year at BCH, I admitted a patient to my ward because I was having trouble controlling his blood pressure as an outpatient. I saw him the morning after admission with a group of medical students. The patient was a tall, thin black male, and his blood pressure had already come down. To my surprise, during my examination, a third-year medical student boldly offered his assessment of the case. He suggested that my patient might have Marfan syndrome, an extremely rare disease that causes connective tissue problems that can result in heart valve abnormalities and aneurysms. It is the type of disease that gung-ho young medical students dream of diagnosing correctly.

Marfan patients are typically tall and thin, with unusually long arms, legs, and fingers. There are specific measurements that can be made to confirm a diagnosis of the syndrome, and so I told my student—trying not to be too defensive—that if he suspected Marfan, then he should take the proper measurements: arm span, distance from the base of the neck to the pubic bone, finger length, and the ratio of height to total arm span.

The next day as I rounded alone in the early morning, I noticed that my patient from the day before was much quieter and more subdued than I had ever seen him.

"What's wrong?" I asked.

"Doc, I know I'm dying. I guess it's time for us to say good-bye."

I glanced at his blood pressure, which was now normal. "Why do you think you're dying?"

"Doc, I know you sent that boy in here to measure me for my pine box!"

Needless to say, I reviewed my student's bedside manner, which in this case involved the extensive use of a tape measure but no communication with the patient whatsoever. The story has always been a source of humor to me, but it also contains an important lesson about communication.

As physicians—trained to be confident, decisive, and knowledgeable—we often fail to explain our actions completely to our patients. Sometimes the result of arrogance or impatience but more often the result of carelessness, miscommunication threatens the quality of medical care a physician can deliver. In order to prevent both the minor mishaps and the fatal errors that can arise through miscommunication, a physician should always aspire to achieve a high level of mutual understanding with his or her patient.

My patient did not have Marfan syndrome, and I have yet to see that disease. But I have seen many more instances where a failure to communicate has led to complications down the line. As the medical profession becomes even faster-paced, with physicians trying to compress patient examinations into fifteen-minute time slots, the potential for doctor-patient misunderstandings has increased. For this reason, I continue to repeat this story—not for the laughs it sometimes gets, but for the important lesson it contains.

While sorrow and humor played a huge role in my education at

BCH, sometimes drama was the vehicle for the personal and professional lessons I learned during residency.

The Boston City Hospital emergency room looked like most
inner-city ERs. It is located in one of the poorest parts of Boston
and serves an area known for violence and crime. As interns in
the ER, we quickly became used to dealing with injuries related
to shootings, car accidents, rape, and trauma. However, though
we witnessed and treated the gruesome results of violence every
day, the hospital was meant to be a place where violent conflict
was resolved, not initiated. However, that was not the case during
one dramatic night in the ER in 1978.

I had spent a quiet evening working the nonacute side of the
house (the section of the ER where less seriously ill patients were
evaluated) when a patient was admitted for vomiting blood. I suspected he was suffering from alcohol-related pancreatitis, and I
ordered a blood test to confirm the diagnosis. The patient had
been drinking, and he was getting more and more agitated
throughout his evaluation. He would almost definitely require
admission, but I was waiting for his lab results. We tried not to
admit patients in the early morning hours because we knew our
fellow house staff would be unlikely to get any rest or sleep except
in the 3:00–5:00 a.m. time slot.

By two o'clock in the morning, this tall, thin, muscular young
man was losing patience with his visit. He was much more interested in where his next drink might come from than what the
results of his amylase test would be. Agitated, he pulled out his
intravenous line and shouted to me that he was leaving. Allowing
him to leave in his condition was not an option. My nurse was on
break, so I was by myself, alone on the quiet side of the ER.

I called for security, and fortunately an officer was readily available. He was an older, balding man in his fifties, perhaps retired

from the police department. His once-imposing physique was now hidden by excessive weight around his midsection. But he was still game and happy to block my patient's exit.

The patient, however, was not to be deterred. A scuffle ensued, and the two became combatants on the floor of the hospital. I watched, unsure what my role should be in this setting. The patient was getting the best of his older, pudgier pursuer, and suddenly I saw hands reaching for the security guard's holster and a gun fall free to the floor.

Instinctively, I jumped into the scene, making it a two-against-one battle. Legs and arms seemed to be moving almost randomly, and there was a good deal of rolling from one position to another. I saw only different body parts and no faces as we grunted and twisted around each other on the floor. The smell of alcohol mixed with the guard's cologne. I lost sight of the loose gun, but at one point it appeared from nowhere, just inches from my face. There was blood everywhere, and though I had not heard a gunshot I wondered if perhaps I might be dying from a gunshot wound. The wrestling match continued for a few long seconds, but ultimately the security guard and I were successful.

The patient was handcuffed and admitted to the locked ward. The blood had come from where the patient had ripped the IV out of his arm. None of it was mine. Nobody was shot or even injured, but my heart was racing and our victory made me feel briefly like a hero. After all, fighting for a gun was not in any intern job description that I knew about. Perhaps I deserved a medal, but a gruff thank you from a shaken, disheveled, and indignant security guard was all I ever got for my exploits. He went back to his post, and I moved on to see the rest of my patients before heading home to sleep until my next shift.

The scuffle was just part of the Boston City Hospital scene. In fact, the danger associated with the loose gun, though dramatic, made so little impact on me that I forgot about it completely over time. The memory of the event, however, would come back to me nearly thirty years later.

2

Kidnapped

On Sunday, March 6, 2005, at around 7:00 a.m., I walked from my bedroom to the kitchen to brew a pot of coffee. My first contact with family was our ten-year-old Australian shepherd, Aussie. She always looked rather comical, with her random and irregular splotches of black, brown, merle, and white and her swaggering gait, the consequence of years of rheumatoid arthritis. That morning she greeted me in the kitchen with a quizzical look and what appeared to be a new toy: a wooden mousetrap holding a pesky mouse that had eluded the family for months. I did not need to be a physician to see that the mouse was dead, probably more from being the dog's snack than from the jaws of the trap itself. So before my morning coffee, the first task of my day was to quickly dispose of the dead mouse. I extracted the corpse from Aussie's mouth with a paper towel and went out through our garage to throw it in the dumpster at the end of our driveway, located in the back alley behind our house.

Glad to be rid of the mouse and perhaps distracted by the general unpleasantness of the situation, I returned to the house without closing the garage, leaving the heavy garage door up and the back door to the house unlocked.

I made myself a cup of coffee and proceeded upstairs to my study, eager to catch up on academic work and return to my Sunday morning routine. My large mahogany desk was a sea of papers, pamphlets, and open books. The floor of the study was strewn with a collection of various medical journals: the white-covered *New England Journal of Medicine,* the red *Journal of Infectious Diseases,* and the blue *Journal of the American Geriatric Society. Harrison's Principles of Internal Medicine,* volumes one and two, were open on the desk, as usual. I had been looking for topics to include in the textbook that I was finishing, a question-and-answer study guide for medical students preparing for their internal medicine clerkship exams.

However, my priority that morning was not medicine but international economics. The night before, my son had e-mailed me a college paper he had written about the effects of outsourcing on the American economy. While I was no expert on the subject, I was always happy to make some suggestions and contributions to Jeremy's work, and he would be eager to have my comments. My wife, Shirley, had already left for church, and my younger son, Justin, was practicing guitar in the basement, about to leave for church as well. The house was quiet, and I became deeply engrossed in reading about the workers in China and India who were taking over American jobs.

At the same time that I was evaluating my son's thoughts on outsourcing, a man in a large, white SUV was turning off Interstate

27 about two miles from my home. He was coming from Lubbock, driving one hundred miles north to Amarillo on a straight and desolate highway flanked by dormant cotton fields, grazing herds of cattle, and isolated metal windmills.

On his way, the man had driven past Plainview, with its dense collection of fast-food stops; past Kress, rumored to have the best pies in the state if you could find its tiny diner; past Tulia, advertised by a single billboard to be a town of the finest people and the richest soil; and on through Canyon, known for the scenic Palo Duro Canyon, the Grand Canyon of Texas.

Amarillo is just eighteen miles north of Canyon. The small city lies at the intersection of I-27 and I-40 and is famous for the Big Texan, a restaurant that offers a free seventy-two-ounce steak dinner to anyone who can eat the entire meal in under an hour. Six minutes from the center of town, the man took Amarillo's Bell Street exit, and within a few minutes he had entered a residential subdivision.

My neighborhood looks typical for a West Texas suburb. The streets are quiet, wide, and tree-lined. Large traditional houses sit well back from the street. Long, even sidewalks lead up through well-manicured lawns to welcome mats and wreath-bound front doors. Down the street from my house is an elementary school; you can see its playground, soccer fields, and even a small greenhouse from my front lawn.

The man avoided the wide streets and the front lawns where neighbors might be chatting or homeowners might be tending their shrubs. Instead, he turned left off of Bell Street down a back alley that leads to the garages and back entrances of private homes. The narrow lane is lined by high wooden fences, which enclose the backyards of my neighbors. These yards are kept perpetually green—despite the arid West Texas climate—by constantly swirling sprinkler systems. As the man drove slowly down the alley, the wheels of his SUV sloshed through puddles of water formed in the uneven pavement. He passed several driveways and slowed down to squeeze by a beige dumpster that now entombed Aussie's unfortunate mouse. Just past the dumpster on the right was a short driveway leading to a two-story, flat-roofed, wooden-shingled house with a three-car garage. A street number was posted on the backyard fence: 4205, my address.

The garage door is open, showing a forest green Chrysler on the left, a white Chevy Blazer on the right, and a vacant spot in the middle where my wife's green minivan is usually parked. The man boldly drives his SUV into the middle space so that there are now two white SUVs parked side by side.

The stranger exits his car clutching a firearm. He passes a collection of tennis rackets on the left wall of the garage and an old campaign sign promoting "Shirley Berk for School Board." There is an extra refrigerator and a dusty bookcase filled with true crime and biography paperbacks. Just before moving into the house through the unlocked back door, he presses a small black button next to the doorframe that triggers the garage door to come down behind him. No one inside the house hears it close, not Justin playing music in the basement, or me reading about China's trade law in the second-floor study.

Once inside, the armed intruder decides to climb the fifteen carpeted stairs immediately to his right. Perhaps as he climbs, he hears the strumming of a guitar coming from the recreation room in the basement below, but he continues to the second floor and comes to a hallway at the top of the stairs. Both walls of the hallway are lined with framed memories and mementos that mean nothing to this man, but each has a special significance in the lives of the people whose home he has just invaded.

There is a black-and-white sketch of an old mustached doctor sitting thoughtfully at his desk: Sir William Osler, the father of internal medicine and one of my personal heroes. My certificates from Phi Beta Kappa and Alpha Omega Alpha hang next to my medical school diploma from Boston University, written entirely in Latin. There is a blue ribbon from my 1992 Boston City Hospital alumni reunion that says "Honorary Chairman." It is flanked in a large commemorative frame by two beautiful old prints of Boston City Hospital from the turn of the century.

Family pictures are everywhere: me with Jeremy, age ten, smiling in front of a replica of the Liberty Bell at Disney World; the 1996 Johnson City Little League team in their blue and gold uniforms, standing proudly with Coach Berk and grinning at their second-place finish; Justin, age two (before his first haircut), smiling while on a family vacation at the beach in Ogunquit, Maine; the entire family (me, Shirley, and the boys) at Palo Duro Canyon, sitting on a stone bench overlooking the majestic canyon below; me, in cap and gown, and my parents at my medical school graduation. There is the picture from a Halloween party we had back in Tennessee: Shirley is wearing a white unicorn costume and I am dressed as a New York Yankee, complete with baseball uniform, batting glove, aviator sunglasses, stripes of black shoe polish under my eyes, and an earring to top it all off. I am young and grinning, with thick black hair and a thin build from running every day.

The stranger does not study these pictures on his way down the hall. He does not think about the people who live in this house and whose memories hang on the wall. He makes his way quickly to the first door on the left, barging into the study where I am intently working on Jeremy's paper.

State of Texas v. Jack Lindsey Jordan

February 2007, Canyon, Texas

JACK LINDSEY JORDAN: I was driving around paranoid. I
came down an alley and into a garage. He was in the study
upstairs. He turned and asked me what I was doing in his
house. I said I was on the run from the police for something
I didn't do. He was scared, extremely scared, and nervous—
and I understood.

There is no warning. The man enters my small office looking
angry and shaking with anxiety. He speaks to me in a low, trembling growl and points a shotgun at my head. His eyes move
wildly in all directions, his deep voice is ominous, and his words
fill the room with doom.

"I will kill you if you don't do what I say."

He is convincing, intimidating, and outrageous. This is terror.
I can feel the physiological symptoms of fear begin to spread
throughout my body, and my thoughts become frantic. There is
no exit, no escape. This is checkmate. No moves, no options, no
hope. I should scream. I should run. I should find something to
throw at him.

In medical school, we were injected with epinephrine in an
experiment that was meant to teach us the functions of the sympathetic nervous system, which is activated when a person en-
counters a sudden threat. The rush I feel now is identical. I have
the same chills and goose bumps. My mouth is dry, and I can feel
myself shaking.

However, at the same time that panic is taking over my body, a
single thought enters my head and prevents me from acting on
my intense feelings of fear: my son Justin is still in the house.

This knowledge becomes clear and vivid in my mind, and somehow allows me to regain focus.

The man pointing a shotgun at my head is aggressive and hostile, but he is also agitated and almost appears frightened himself. His obvious anxiety makes him all the more dangerous and terrifying to me. I try to gain control of myself and the situation. An inner voice, well-disciplined and experienced, gives counsel. *Take a deep breath and live one second at a time.*

"Do you have any guns in the house?"

"No, I do not." The words are pushed out past a dry tongue. *Stay calm. Stay focused. Maintain control of yourself and the situation.*

"Is there anyone else in the house?"

"I have a son who may still be home."

My panic subsides somewhat as I answer his questions, and I try to take stock of this unknown intruder. He is about five foot nine and maybe one hundred and eighty pounds, with dark hair and a beard of stubble. I have never seen him before, and I try to make some sense of who he might be. His face is round, his features symmetrical. He has a boyish look, despite the crow's feet around his eyes, which are blue and bloodshot. He wears a brightly striped button-down shirt and jeans. He is irritable, and with the shotgun aimed at my head, he is painfully terrifying.

The shotgun he holds is the greatest cause of my fear. It holds the potential for the type of calamity and suffering that I have seen firsthand on countless nights in the emergency room: injury, trauma, disfigurement, painful rehabilitation, and worst of all, sudden death. I know the type of damage this gun will do to my body at such close range. There will be an explosive skull rupture, projectile brain material, and a gaping exit wound. I frighten myself with my memories of patients coming in with gunshot wounds and begin to contemplate becoming one of the many unfortunate victims of violence and crime. Instead of succumbing to fear, however, I try to achieve the same calm with which I approached those very situations.

All physicians practice the art of performing optimally during emergencies. One of the most important skills a doctor can perfect is maintaining composure under pressure. Throughout my career in medicine, I have written, studied, and taught about Sir William Osler, a physician and educator who practiced at the turn of the twentieth century. Osler is famous for his essay on aequanimitas—the ability to remain calm and rational. Osler argues that above all, a physician should be composed and logical in every situation.

In 1983, when I was a professor of medicine at East Tennessee State University, my students performed a skit about my making rounds at the hospital and getting my instructions directly from Osler in heaven. "Steve," said the deep voice of Osler, "I know you will calmly teach these students what to do in this emergency." A black-wigged student, my look-alike, maintained a stoic calm throughout the calamities that followed: malfunctioning equipment, simultaneous cardiac arrests, urgent phone calls, disoriented residents, and distracted nurses. The skit portrayed a very calculating and unemotional Dr. Berk.

Yes, I am practically staring down the barrel of a very dangerous weapon, in the hands of a very agitated intruder, but I must keep my composure. I commit myself to equanimity, to emotional control, to rationality, clear thinking, optimism, and good judgment. My biggest concern is the safety of my seventeen-year-old son. I feel that special worry reserved for one's children, which tightens the stomach, captures the heartbeat.

State of Texas v. Jack Lindsey Jordan

> JACK LINDSEY JORDAN: He said I think my son is still in the
> house. And I said well, I don't want to meet him. And he
> said well, I don't want you to meet him.

I tell him that my son is downstairs and that he will be leaving soon. There is no discussion, but it is clear that both of us want him out of the house. The man uses his gun to direct me out of the study and down the stairs. With his gun in my back, he follows me into the laundry room, which is across from the back door that leads out to our garage. My son will not be able to see us here when he comes upstairs. We wait in silence for him to leave.

The gunman stands against the back wall and I stand facing the laundry room entrance. The shotgun is between us, its barrel pressed into the small of my back. The small room is tense and crowded. We are packed in tightly with the washing machine, dryer, and sink. I notice the tile floor and the empty dog food bowl and try to process what is happening on this strange Sunday morning, which is suddenly ablaze with the overt threat of violence.

We wait. I cannot tell how long, for time loses all meaning in a crisis. I worry about what will happen if Justin sees us. What if he panics or tries to be heroic? I am convinced that if he becomes at all involved in the situation, he will be killed. I cannot imagine this desperate man dealing with two captives, and I do not want to find out what he might do in a two-on-one situation. I think the only way to protect Justin is to keep him from getting involved. My only goal is to make sure he leaves the house without suspecting that anything is wrong. We wait.

Eventually, we hear my son come upstairs from the game room below. The man does not move but continues to point his gun at me when I stick my head out the door of the laundry room. Justin would not have expected to see me there, since I never do laundry. I tell him good-bye and that I know he is off to church, doing my best to sound nonchalant and busy, though I am certain my voice sounds cracked and strained. *Leave by the front door,* I wish anxiously to myself. I do not want Justin to exit through the garage and see the captor as he passes the laundry room.

Miraculously, Justin doesn't question why I am standing in the laundry room, doesn't notice that my voice sounds strange. There is no reason for him to pick up on these details. Why should anyone be suspicious in his own home on a typical Sunday morning? He doesn't pause, but calls out good-bye and leaves through the front door, meeting a friend who is waiting there to pick him up rather than driving to church by himself. The door slams shut, and I know he is safe.

I'm exhilarated that I have kept him from becoming entangled in this predicament. I thank God that he did not see his father in this humiliating position, that he will not bear the scars of witnessing a crime in his own house. He was just a few feet away from this armed intruder, but now he is safe. Relieved, I briefly lament that I wasn't able to properly say good-bye. I wonder for a painful moment if I'll ever see him again. That thought is terrifying.

Once we are sure my son is gone, we step out of the laundry room. Having spent long moments in tense silence, the intruder now gets more threatening, and his shotgun actually touches my face as he explains what he wants from me.

"I'm on the run from the law. I want cash and that's all."

He holds his weapon as if he would be happy for me to give

him a reason to use it. I remember how well I survived my emergency room scuffle, but I have no interest in being a hero. I have no thought of running or calling for help. I just want him gone, and so I immediately begin searching for money.

I find my wallet and hand him all the money I have inside: three twenty-dollar bills. He angrily tells me that sixty dollars is not enough. I get defensive. We do not have a safe or a stash of cash in the house. I do not have the money that he needs.

"Is there any more money anywhere in the house?" He asks the question in a quiet voice, as if to say, There'd better be.

I tell him that we might find some money in my son's room upstairs; so we head back up to the second floor, again with the gun to my back. We go down the hallway, past the study to Justin's room. I am glad to show the stranger this room. It is full of family photographs, sports trophies, and other signs of youthful vitality that I hope will inspire him to be merciful. I want the room to say, "You are an intruder. Your gun does not belong here. Perhaps you have your own children or remember good times with your own dad." I want the room to say, "You must not harm this father."

The man is not interested in family artifacts. He continues to demand money and threaten me with his gun as I search my son's room. I find almost one hundred dollars in the nightstand, but it is still not enough. The man is committing armed robbery, but it is not paying off. He wants more. He gets angry, mean, condescending, and irritable. Clearly he blames me for making things more complicated. I suspect he is thinking, *You don't have enough money, so things are going to be more difficult for both of us.*

We leave my son's room and head back downstairs. I begin to wonder what he will do with me. Perhaps he will shoot me and leave. He directs me toward the garage, and suddenly I break into a cold sweat. *Don't put me in the car trunk.* The thought causes a rush of real fear. I would prefer to run for it, if it comes to that. I will run across the large field near my house, and get shot down with the open sky and the sun above me.

He tells me to get the garage door opener out of my car and then directs me into the driver's seat of his SUV. He gets into the back seat and points the barrel of his shotgun into my side. "We're going to a bank machine and you're going to get me at least five hundred dollars!" I open the garage and start the car, pulling out of the secluded back alley of our house and onto Bell Street.

It is a beautiful spring day in a city that I have come to love, and I have been kidnapped.

3

Getting to Amarillo

When I finished my residency at Boston City Hospital in 1979, I never thought my career would take me to Amarillo, Texas. Up to that point, I thought I was on a path to become a missionary doctor. I had wanted to be a physician since junior high school, when I read the work of Thomas Dooley, a U.S. naval officer and doctor who wrote eloquently about his years of service in Vietnam and Laos in the 1950s. Inspired by his dedication and selfless service to the unfortunate, I decided to become a missionary myself, and imagined treating barefoot children and adult have-nots in the remotest areas of the world, places of isolation and poverty where only idealistic young doctors like me would ever choose to go.

I continued to dream of missionary work in college at Brandeis University, where I majored in anthropology. I wanted to learn about a wide range of human behaviors and beliefs and hoped that my studies would prepare me to work closely with patients from many different backgrounds and cultures. In medical school, my decision to spend my fourth year on the Indian reservation at Keams fit perfectly with my long-term plans.

However, during my three years at BCH, I began drifting toward academic medicine. I still planned to return to Keams Canyon and pursue a career of service in other impoverished regions of the world, but I also developed a keen interest in infectious disease and clinical research. Many of my mentors were in academic medicine, devoted not only to treating patients, but also to teaching new physicians and conducting research that would develop and improve the way doctors practiced medicine in the future. Boston had some of the greatest academic physicians in the country, especially in infectious disease: William McCabe, Jerry Klein, John Bartlett, Dick Gleckman, Louis Weinstein, and Maxwell Finland, the grandfather of the field of infectious disease.

When I arrived at BCH in 1975, Dr. Finland was close to retirement. An immigrant from the Ukraine, Dr. Finland was less than five feet tall, white-haired, and shy. During his career, which spanned well over half a century, he pioneered studies of infectious organisms and the antibiotics used to treat them. In the 1930s, his work studying sulfadiazine and penicillin as treatments for pneumonia cut the mortality rate for that disease by two-thirds. For a resident like me, this hero of infectious disease was approachable by appropriate protocol, and my proximity to greatness was an appealing aspect of training at BCH. As luck would have it, however, three years into my residency, I got to know Dr. Finland much more personally than most other fellows in my program.

On February 6, 1978, I was working in the infectious disease laboratory of BCH, conducting an experiment on sepsis in mice. The procedure—injecting various concentrations of bacteria and antibody into different veins of dozens of mice—was extremely tedious and required intense concentration, and I had become so preoccupied that I failed to leave before the blizzard hit.

That evening, Boston was covered with twenty-seven inches of snowfall. It was the Great Blizzard of '78, and I was trapped overnight in the deserted laboratory of Boston City Hospital. Alone, I could hear the muffled sound of scurrying animals coming from the walls: a rodent infestation or perhaps the descendants of small lab animals that had escaped their cages over the decades of research that had been conducted in that historic building. After passing several hours alone, I heard the more comforting sound of human footsteps in the hallway. It was Dr. Finland, also stranded by the storm, coming down to the lab from his office on the second floor.

After brief introductions (though of course, I knew who *he* was) we decided to check out the fridge in the break room. For the next hour or so, over cold leftovers, we discussed the various research projects going on in the infectious disease department. I was interested in studying a bacterium called pneumococcus, but Dr. Finland suggested I pursue a project studying coagulase negative staphylococcus instead. I did not follow his suggestion, since at the time I was uninterested in the organism (thought to be a lab contaminant in many blood cultures). That strain of staph is now known to be one of the most common causes of sepsis.

Though I missed out on that particular opportunity, I did maintain a professional relationship with Max long after the night of that blizzard. Three years later, my paper on pneumococcal pericarditis appeared in the *American Journal of Medicine* with Dr. Finland as the senior author. Having the opportunity to work with and learn from a legend like Max Finland was a huge step on my path toward academic medicine. I was impressed by his dedication to his profession, and especially to his students. He believed strongly that the future of medicine could only be ensured through careful research of new treatments, bedside diagnosis, and diligent training of new physicians, and he gave himself equally to these pursuits. I had been inspired by Dooley's selflessness, but the passion of Boston City Hospital's attending physicians was no less compelling, and throughout my residency and fellowship, I was drawn more and more toward academic medicine.

Another factor in my shift toward academia was the realization that I loved to teach. Throughout my training at BCH, I enjoyed having medical students and interns accompany me on rounds. It was thrilling to see the process of discovery and the development of confidence in my peers. And I was a good teacher. Medical students from Harvard and Boston University would sign up for electives if they found out that I was the fellow on rotation. For the rest of my career the opportunity to teach a medical student something valuable and enduring was exhilarating.

By the time I had to decide where I would go after my training, practicing in an underdeveloped country no longer seemed realistic. I wondered how I would care for patients without the technology that I had come to depend on. And more importantly, I did not have the religious convictions that were part of most medical missions abroad. I did apply to the Indian Health Service, hoping to return to Arizona, but they were only hiring primary care physicians, and I had chosen to specialize in infectious disease. I began to consider my other options.

Both Boston University and Harvard provided opportunities for infectious disease instructors, but there were so many of us in Boston that we were totally dispensable. Those who signed on with Harvard might stay at the lowly instructor level for five years or more, performing the least desirable clinical rotations, working in someone else's laboratory, organizing conferences, and running the slide projector. I did not want to spend the next five years fetching lunches for the senior faculty at the sandwich truck parked between the Boston City Hospital emergency room and the Laboratory for Infectious Diseases.

I found an alternative in a new medical school being established in eastern Tennessee. The region was in desperate need of physicians, and the medical school at East Tennessee State University (ETSU) was established specifically to train physicians who would ultimately work in the underserved region of Appalachia, where the rural population was as much in need of doctors as some underdeveloped countries. The school was looking for young, well-trained faculty for the new medical school campus in Johnson City, and I was looking for a place where I would make a difference and have opportunities for advancement in the future. I had never been south of Atlantic City and I hardly knew where Johnson City was, but I loaded up my car, left Boston, and never looked back. At a good-bye party my chief announced, "Dr. Berk is going to be a Tennessee volunteer." Completely unaware that Tennessee is known as "the Volunteer State," I could only think to say, "No, I'll be getting paid."

East Tennessee was as close to missionary work as I would ever do. The East Tennessee State University Quillen School of Medicine is on the grounds of the Veterans Administration Medical Center. It was one of five Teague-Cranston medical schools— schools that were established by Congress in association with a veterans hospital. The several acres of the campus are mostly green fields. East Tennessee is lush with foliage and trees of all kinds, especially dogwoods, which line the street across from old brick buildings with elaborate gargoyles. There is a clock tower, a medical history library, and buildings that house patients at all levels of care: acute hospital, nursing home, domiciliary. Each building has its own number—including number 99, the outhouse adjacent to the softball field. There's a lake where children would come to feed the ducks until the 1990s, when sunbathing, fishing, and duck feeding became out of control and were banned because the activities were inconsistent with a busy medical center. An ornately decorated wooden gazebo, prominent in a large field adjacent to the medical school building, was used on Sundays for weddings. The Boy Scouts were permitted to camp out on the medical center fields and would decorate the on-campus cemetery with a flag on each grave on Memorial Day.

Many of the patients I saw in Johnson City were from the most rural, impoverished, and uneducated regions of Appalachia. As an infectious disease specialist (I was appointed chief of the division in 1982), I saw some of Tennessee's first AIDS cases and struggled alongside the victims who succumbed to the disease before adequate treatment options became available. It was a challenging and important time for physicians in infectious disease, as the field surpassed oncology in the area of end-of-life care.

In addition to treating patients, I continued pursuing academic medicine and enjoyed teaching talented, enthusiastic young students and residents. I developed close relationships with my students, and all graduating classes of the ETSU School of Medicine honored me with a teaching award at their graduation ceremony. I quickly rose through the ranks, and in 1988 I was appointed chairman of medicine, a position I held for eleven years.

However, during the years I spent in Johnson City, my greatest personal accomplishment was raising a family. In 1979 I met

Shirley, an East Tennessee native. We were married in 1981 and had two boys, Jeremy and Justin, shortly after. From then on, Shirley and I were a team, raising our sons and watching with wonder as they passed from helpless infancy into precocious childhood. I loved coming home to dinner with my family and hearing all about the new things the boys were learning at school. When I was not on call, I spent my weekends playing with the boys, coaching Jeremy's little league team or Justin's flag football team. (Justin grabbed the coveted quarterback position because he was the only one who could remember the plays.) Nothing made me more proud than to see them grow up with the strong values that Shirley and I shared from the beginning.

Over twenty years, I established both a career and a family in Johnson City. In 1997, I had tremendous support from students and colleagues to become the dean of ETSU College of Medicine, but the university president, whose career I had helped promote, opposed my candidacy. I liked Tennessee, but I knew then that it was time to move on. I was at a point in my career where I wanted to contribute not just to the operations of a medical school, but to its vision. I still enjoyed seeing patients and teaching students, but I also wanted new challenges after twenty years of being a physician. The day I was passed over for dean, the dinnertime conversation was subdued as Shirley and I discussed the politics of academic medicine. The discussion prompted Justin to ask, "Dad, which is higher, a dean or a doctor?" Foolishly I quickly answered, "a dean." Justin, then nine years old, responded, "Wow, I didn't think there was anything higher than a doctor."

I began to look for opportunities elsewhere. I heard about an opening for the regional deanship at Texas Tech University School of Medicine in Amarillo, Texas.

A Boston University School of Medicine classmate, Dr. Edward Sherwood, was the director of a biotech company, Amarillo Bioscience, that was working on new treatments for infectious diseases. Several years before the deanship vacancy, Ed had asked me to serve as the chairman of the advisory board. This required annual visits to Amarillo. When I went there with Shirley, we both agreed that it was a wonderful city. We spent a day at Palo Duro Canyon, just twenty miles south of town, and it reminded me of the Indian reservation in Arizona, a Grand Canyon right outside the city. Some people have the impression that West Texas might as well be another planet. But to me, Amarillo was a city of wide-open spaces, friendly people, and spectacular scenery. Some fall in love with Amarillo quickly and some more gradually. I was among the former. I applied for the position and became the regional dean. I never missed the rolling hills, grasses, and trees of East Tennessee or the great cosmopolitan cities of New York or Boston.

My work in Amarillo was exactly the challenge I was looking for. There were serious problems with the medical school campus when I moved there with my family in 1999. In fact, just weeks before I arrived, the president of Texas Tech was considering closing the Amarillo campus of the medical school because of tension between the school and the local community. But I had helped build a medical school from the ground up in Johnson City, and now ETSU was a leader in primary care. So I was not discouraged, and over time the Texas Tech campus at Amarillo grew rapidly and improved its reputation. In five years, our teaching hospital almost doubled in faculty and revenue. We expanded the school's research programs, successfully establishing projects in cancer, women's health, and geriatrics. The teaching program became the best of all Texas Tech campuses; students graduating from Amarillo were getting the highest exam scores in their clerkships and giving Amarillo the highest ratings in our student satisfaction surveys. I brought some great people with me from East Tennessee, convinced some of the best doctors in the community to join the medical school, and established a group of department chairs who were loyal to me and enthusiastic about bringing positive change to the campus.

Our success in expanding the medical school was extremely gratifying, but equally rewarding was the fact that my work brought me closer to the people of Amarillo. Perhaps because of their frontier roots, the people of this area were hardworking, progressive, and dedicated to their community. As regional dean, I worked to build collaborative efforts between the medical school and the city, and I was always looking for other ways to make personal contributions to the community. For example, I agreed to chair fund-raising walks—for the March of Dimes, American Diabetes Association, and Alzheimer's Association—all in the same year. My wife became active at the schools our sons attended, and was highly involved in the citywide PTA. I liked Amarillo from the moment I arrived, and I worked hard to become a part of the strong community there. I was born in New York City, reared in New Jersey, trained in Boston, and married in Johnson City. But Amarillo was the only place that felt like home. After six years of living there, I felt settled and peaceful in a town that I had grown to know and love.

On a Sunday morning in 2005, I am driving a stranger's SUV down the streets of my neighborhood. The sun is shining (as it does in Amarillo 340 days of the year), but today it is glaring, perhaps because fear has dilated my pupils and literally opened my eyes. My abductor is sitting behind me with his shotgun in the small of my back. I am trying to take one moment at a time. I remind myself that my family is safe. I tell myself that I can survive this ordeal.

The gunman directs me where to go. We are looking for an ATM machine, but he is a stranger to Amarillo and his directions have taken us into a residential area. I follow his instructions without questioning, having no desire to upset him further. He tells me to turn onto Bell Street, and we pass Amarillo High, where both my sons attended high school. At three o'clock on a weekday, this road would be congested with sports cars and pick-up trucks escaping from the school's parking lots with the sound of hip-hop blaring from their windows. On a Sunday morning, however, the high school parking lots and athletic fields are abandoned.

Bell Street is a wide, quiet street dotted with various shops, strip malls, apartment complexes, and fast-food restaurants. Today, there are very few cars on the road. Within several miles, we drive past the Paramount Baptist Church, Church of Latter Day Saints, Southwest Church of Christ, Church of God, West View Christian Church, and Unitarian Universalist Church. All of them are holding services. When we pass by the Bell Avenue Baptist Church, I read its billboard message of inspiration: *Do not be terrified; do not be discouraged, for the LORD your God will be with you wherever you go.* The church's white steeple reaches up into the sky, as if to suggest from where my help would come.

In his search for an ATM, my abductor has become even more agitated. We see several machines in front of the Amarillo National Bank, but these are not acceptable to him. He wants a machine that is more isolated, so we continue driving. His erratic directions take us back into a residential area, and he begins to exhibit even more signs of his paranoia. He watches me very closely and questions my driving at every opportunity.

"Look in your rearview mirror! See if someone is following us. Take that right." Several moments later: "He's still there. Do you know him?"

"No, I don't," I answer.

"Take the next left."

Perhaps I am influenced by his paranoia, for I begin to worry myself that maybe Justin has gotten wind of something and is trying to follow us. But there is no one behind us, and we continue driving, once again turning onto Bell Street. Eventually we find a credit union ATM that he likes. It stands alone near the corner of Bell and Thirty-fourth Street, a bright turquoise and white box with ATM written in large letters across the top. It is next to the curb and shaded by a tall oak tree, separated from a strip mall by an expansive parking lot. I pull up to the machine, which has a small screen and a panel of colored buttons on the right with a slot below for withdrawing cash. How pleased I would be to have that slot pour forth money so that this man could take what he wanted and then be on his way to somewhere else.

I tell him that I have never used a machine like this, that my wife always gets the money for both of us. From the car, I press a button that says my transaction will be in English, not Spanish. So far so good. But when the machine requests a PIN number, I am at a loss. I did not even know ATMs used PIN numbers. I would be all too happy to access my account and withdraw as much cash as it would take to satisfy this gunman and get him out of my life, but I have no idea what to do and neither does he. He gets frustrated and complains that he has abducted the world's stupidest person.

In 2009, seventeen-year-old Linda Burk (spelled with a *u* and no relation to me) also had not used an ATM machine before. She was kidnapped in Los Angeles by drug-addicted Charlie Samuel, who had just violated parole. Burk was ordered by Samuel to drive him to an ATM machine in her black Volvo. A surveillance camera showed repeated unsuccessful attempts to get cash. Over the course of the next hour Burk called both her parents asking them for instructions on how to use the card. She did not let on that she was in trouble, stating only that she needed to buy shoes. When she found out that the card could not be used for such transactions, she told her father she would be coming home to get money. She never made it home. Several hours later, Burk was found in the passenger seat, dead of traumatic head injuries. During Samuel's trial, it was determined that he had committed a similar crime years before, forcing an elderly San Bernardino man to withdraw cash from an ATM machine and threatening to kill him if he reported the crime.

If I am able to get him cash, I believe my abductor will let me get out of the car and drive away. But it will not be that simple.

At a loss, I tell him that perhaps my wife has left a PIN number in my wallet. While we are still parked beside the ATM, I take it out of my pocket and we look through it together, as if we are two partners in crime. It is already empty of cash, but he finds a Texas Tech ID badge and realizes that I am a physician. He sees several credit cards and is attracted to the two that are from Texas Tech, issued by the State of Texas. He pulls out a small index card, folded and creased, with faded blue horizontal lines. It is something that has been in my wallet for years, a quote from Robert Frost that Tom Dooley had carried with him on his missions to Southeast Asia, and which I had copied to keep with me as well.

> The woods are lovely, dark and deep,
>
> But I have promises to keep,
>
> And miles to go before I sleep.

I have carried this card since college, but this abductor is probably the first person to see it. It reminds me of the admiration I had for Tom Dooley, a man who gave up comfort and security in his home in St. Louis to pursue humanitarian work with sick children in Southeast Asia. It reminds me of my own obligation as a physician: to make sacrifices for my patients, to commit to causes beyond my own self-interests, to persevere in doing what I believe is right. I wonder if the message written on that card, which has meant so much to me over the years, means anything to this stranger. He reads it without comment and returns it to me.

Finding no PIN number in my wallet, he suggests that I call my wife and get the information we need from her. This leads to the longest discussion we have had so far. We consider what we should do to get him money, what will work and what will not. I tell him that I would prefer not to be in confrontation with the police, and we establish our common goal: get him what he wants so we can head our separate ways.

I tell him that calling my wife at church and asking for a PIN number would be too suspicious, too out of the ordinary. He says, "Tell her you're going out for a good time with the boys."

I haven't been to a bar since college. The last beer I had was the day after we hosted a party for medical students. I came in from a run and the lone bottle in the refrigerator was the last cold beverage we had in the house. "No, that would make no sense to her. I don't have good times like that."

"You know, going out to drink some beers."

We're from different worlds, and I try to explain that his plan will not work. But he insists that I make the phone call. We begin driving around again, this time in search of a pay phone. (I have not brought my cell phone with me.) We find one in the back of a shopping center, but he is worried about letting me out of the car to cross the parking lot alone.

State of Texas v. Jack Lindsey Jordan

DISTRICT ATTORNEY BLOUNT: So you and the doctor were in your car and you were driving around. Is that correct?

JACK LINDSEY JORDAN: Yes. He was driving.

BLOUNT: Where did you go?

JORDAN: We went to an ATM machine.

BLOUNT: What was the purpose of going to the ATM machine?

JORDAN: To get some money for gas.

BLOUNT: Were you able to get money from the ATM machine?

JORDAN: No sir.

BLOUNT: Why is that?

JORDAN: He didn't know his PIN number.

BLOUNT: Did you get upset about that?

JORDAN: No. I think I made a comment to him . . . I said something to the effect, you don't even know how to use an ATM machine.

BLOUNT: Once you left the ATM machine, where did you go?

JORDAN: We went to a telephone. He was going to call his wife at church.

BLOUNT: Did he ever call his wife?

JORDAN: No, he said he would rather not.

BLOUNT: Where did you go after that?

JORDAN: Riding around.

As we continue our circuitous drive through Amarillo, I notice a sticker in the lower left corner of the windshield. It is the vehicle registration number, ten numbers and four letters.

When I was in eighth grade, my Spanish teacher taught us a lesson on memorization. "Concentration is what is important," said the teacher (a young man who was not interested in Spanish at all). He proposed an exercise: we were given a set of numbers to memorize, starting with six digits and getting longer as the rounds went on. It was like a spelling bee: miss your series and you're out.

I was the winner. Long after everyone else had been eliminated, I continued to recite the numbers he gave me until I finally made a mistake on a series that was eighteen digits long. I remember dividing the series into groups of three, relating them to batting averages, homeroom numbers, and grade-point averages. The teacher said, "Okay, Steve, now do them backwards." But backwards or forwards, it was the same to me.

State of Texas v. Jack Lindsey Jordan

> DISTRICT ATTORNEY BLOUNT: Did you obtain some identification number from Dr. Berk?
>
> GARY NABORS, AMARILLO POLICE DEPARTMENT: Dr. Berk told me that he was forced to drive the vehicle while the suspect sat in the back seat. While he was driving the vehicle he had memorized the number off the back sticker on the left lower windshield. When we ran that, it came up on our computer as the suspect's vehicle.
>
> BLOUNT: Officer, I'm going to show you state exhibit number 15. Is there some identification number in that photo?
>
> NABORS: Yes sir. It's right below the bar code.

BLOUNT: And how does that compare with the number that
    Dr. Berk gave to you that day?
NABORS: It's very close, with the exception of the zero on the
    front.

Perhaps I do not know how to use an ATM, but I have a special
skill, which has suddenly become useful. *You are a stranger,* I
think to myself, *invading my home without invitation or introduc-
tion. I have no idea where you have come from, who you are, what you
will do to me or where you will go. But you now have a number, a
number that distinguishes you from others.*

We continue to drive aimlessly in search of a pay phone. He
asks me what kind of a doctor I am, briefly making eye contact
with me in the rearview mirror, something he has not done up to
this point. I tell him that I'm an internist who cares for all patients, rich and poor, patients with all kinds of problems. I've always been there for people with drug problems, mental problems, those who can't pay.

Surprisingly, he wants to tell me about himself. He's become
addicted to pain meds since being in prison, and he uses methamphetamines. In fact, he would like to stop at a pharmacy and
have me get amphetamines from the pharmacist.

"Tell them your aunt is too fat and needs amphetamines."

Like churches, pharmacies are abundant on Bell Street, but I
convince him that neither CVS nor United Supermarkets will let
us just drop in for amphetamines.

He asks me if I have drugs at my house, and I tell him that I
don't. He suggests that surely I must have doctor friends who
have drugs at their home.

"Why don't we visit them?"

I picture a few colleagues and imagine their reaction to a surprise visit from the dean and his new, drug-addicted acquaintance.

"Drug addiction is a medical problem," I tell him.

He doesn't reply, but he drops the pharmacy idea. I suspect he knows it's not wise.

We have been driving for well over half an hour, and suddenly he realizes that we need to fill up with gas. Abandoning the search for a telephone, we are now looking for a gas station. Again, his distraction and paranoia prevent this from being an easy task. We pass several stations before he decides on a corner Shell and tells me to pull up at the pump farthest from the building. He gives me my Texas Tech purchasing card, which I'm specifically forbidden to use to pay for gas. This will be hard to explain to the auditors. I suggest my personal card instead, but he is adamant; he likes the state card. I get out of the car and begin to fill up.

For the first time, there is a potential for escape. I can run to the pay station and ask for help. The other pumps are empty, but there should be at least one clerk inside the building. Perhaps I'm just too fearful, but I don't take the chance. I think about the gun he has been pointing at me for the past hour. I don't know much about shotguns or rifles, and I wonder how fast they're ready to shoot.

Before I finish filling the tank, another car drives into the station. My abductor gets spooked and demands that I get back in the car. I quickly close the gas tank and drive away.

The man is angry and frustrated. We have been driving for an hour and have accomplished nothing.

"Drive back to your house."

"I can't do that because my wife will be home by now," I explain to him.

He insists, and I begin to lose the composure I have kept up until this point. The plan was to get him money so he would let me go. But now he wants me to take him back to my house. I begin to panic at the thought of taking him anywhere near my family again.

A cold sweat overcomes me. I plead with him to let me go. I have one episode of a dry heave. He asks if I'm okay but remains adamant and angry that I would disobey him. He says that he doesn't want to hurt me or my wife. He will take our jewelry and my wife's wallet, and then let me go. It's his new plan, and he wants no more discussion from me.

There's nothing I can do. I drive down the streets that lead us back to my house. After all that wandering, we're still only a few miles away. In less than ten minutes, I am driving down the alley, pulling past the dumpster, and turning into the driveway of my house. We are back where we started.

"Open the garage door," he demands gruffly.

I had brought the garage door opener with me like he asked and put it between my legs on the front seat. But now it's not there.

"Open the door." His voice rises and reflects his impatience. He knows I didn't want to return.

"I can't find the garage door opener," I reply, my voice trembling. I know he will think I'm trying to fool or disobey him, but in fact the garage door opener is gone.

He says that I'm lying. The shotgun touches my head. It is his weapon of intimidation and he manipulates it for maximum power. He instills terror in my very core. Our heartbeats increase and our faces both flush. I feel mine and see his.

"Open the damn door. I'm going to kill you, right here."

I believe him. He is red-faced and yelling now. I have not and would not purposefully disobey him. He is impulsive. His life has likely been a long series of perpetual frustrations, and this morning has been frustration beyond capacity. I feel like I'm in a nightmare. As a doctor, I am an old acquaintance of death, but have never really contemplated my own. Until now.

4

The Thin Line

I n my career and in my personal life, I have seen death in all
its forms: anticipated, sudden, violent, peaceful, sad, and inspiring. I have seen people confront death in every possible
manner, and I can recall their expressions of peaceful anticipa-
tion, noble courage and defiance, fear, resolve, relief, and even
joy. I can picture the faces of men and women who died without
warning and others who clearly saw death coming, but survived.
I have witnessed tragedy and miraculous recovery, and I am
keenly aware of the fine line between life and death.

With the barrel of a gun pressed into my temple, I consider the
truth of this cliché with vivid and terrifying clarity. I am on that
thin wavering line, hanging by that figurative thread, walking
that figurative tightrope, with a dark unknown abyss below. I
close my eyes and think about death.

In 1971, I was a counselor at a summer camp in northeast New
Jersey. Camp Merry Heart had all the features of a typical sum-

mer camp: six rustic cabins arranged around a football-sized field, with an American flag flying in the center. There was a mess hall, a nature cabin, an arts and crafts center, a pool, and a small man-made lake. The only difference between Camp Merry Heart and any other summer camp was that all of the nature trails at Merry Heart were wide enough to accommodate a wheelchair. The entire campus was specially designed for its handicapped and disabled campers.

The children and young adults who attended Camp Merry Heart had a range of afflictions. There were many cases of muscular dystrophy and cerebral palsy, but also other more unusual neurological disorders and several severe cases of autism. But the children did not come to be pitied. They were there to have a good time and—as much as possible—do what other children do at camp. There was swimming, color war, a carnival-themed field day, and even under-control panty raids and food fights. But as typical as we tried to make the experience for our campers, being a counselor at Camp Merry Heart had its unique challenges.

Each cabin held twenty campers and was kept spotlessly clean. As counselors, we mopped the wooden floors, scrubbed the bathrooms, folded up pajamas and tucked them neatly under pillows. The cabins smelled of ammonia in the morning, but an odor of urine or worse might prevail by evening. The mess hall accommodated all one hundred or so handicapped children at the same time. Mealtime was loud, crowded, and chaotic, with counselors running back and forth between the food line and the tables, serving seconds and clearing trays. Some counselors were assigned to work one-on-one with the children who were too handicapped to feed themselves. A "feeder" would sit next to his or her charge throughout dinner, patiently spoon-feeding macaroni and cheese or rice pudding to the camper's mouth. Kept constantly busy, most counselors did not get a chance to eat at dinnertime, but there was always food available for us after the campers had gone to sleep.

That summer of 1971 was my seventh and final summer at Camp Merry Heart. (I was starting medical school at Boston University in the fall.) As the oldest and most experienced counselor, I was assigned the most physically challenged campers, a role I took great pride in. That summer I was charged to help two close friends of mine, Pat Goldy and Kevin Spark, who, like me, had been coming to camp for years.

Pat and Kevin both suffered from Duchenne-type muscular dystrophy, a genetic disorder that causes rapid muscle degeneration, the loss of ambulation, and ultimately, death. Most patients do not live past the age of twenty. At the age of seventeen, Pat and Kevin were both confined to wheelchairs, having lost the ability to walk years before and now barely able to move their arms and legs at all. Pat had blond hair and sat tall in his long-backed wheelchair. Kevin was smaller, with brown hair and freckles. He sat hunched over slightly, a result of the osteoporosis that had developed secondary to his muscular dystrophy.

My campers were quiet, intelligent, and reflective, and I tried to design a schedule especially suited to them. We learned to use a shortwave radio and would listen for hours, searching for broadcasts from around the world. Each time we got a transmission from a new country, we would fill out a report and send it to that country's radio station to receive a QSL card documenting that we had indeed received their signal. We collected stamps. Each boy had an inexpensive album and a small bag full of international stamps, more than enough work for a single summer. We played chess. Kevin could still move the pieces slowly on his own, and I would move for Pat.

Sometimes we would take excursions outdoors. I would re-cruit another counselor to help me navigate their wheelchairs down the narrow dirt path to the lake, avoiding every possible bump in the road. We had invented a simple method of fishing. I built a large wooden box with a wire-mesh bottom. I would drop the box down into the water and the boys would scatter bread-crumbs over the top. After waiting for some sign of movement in the water, I would pull the box up quickly and hope to find a guppy. After a successful day, the boys would write home, "We caught some fish at the lake today."

Usually, however, we just sat under a tree in the humid New Jersey sunshine. The boys preferred the quiet activities and gen-erally avoided the younger, more active campers. We talked a lot, and sometimes they would embarrass me by asking questions about this or that female counselor, who had a boyfriend and who might be available. In many ways, they were completely normal teenagers.

Pat and Kevin were good-natured and fun to be with, but tak-ing care of them was a twenty-four-hour job. Nighttime was par-ticularly challenging. Neither boy could move his legs or shift position at night. At home, they depended on their parents for almost constant nighttime supervision. At camp, I told them that they could call me at night whenever they needed their legs moved or their face scratched. I told them I didn't mind, although it was difficult for me to wake up so often and still function the next day. They told me they didn't want the other boys, most of whom were ambulatory and didn't share their problem, to hear them. To make sure they would never hesitate to call me, I set up a signaling device that Kevin could use just by pressing a lever that set off a quiet beep in the cubicle where I slept. (Counselors slept in the cabin with the campers, but our beds were separated from the main room by a thin screen for privacy.) Their beds were close and the screen was insubstantial, so usually I would hear them talking well before they signaled for my help.

"I think I'm going to need Mr. Steve to move my foot."

"Well, I need some help with my blanket, so we can call him together."

"Or we can wait. I'll probably need him to move my pillow soon."

I would smile to myself and just happen to stop by at the right time.

Through their years of camp together and their intimately shared experiences, Pat and Kevin had developed an extremely close relationship. They were soul mates, and I could hear them talking together late into the night. One night I overheard a conversation that I would never forget.

"I think this is our last summer at camp," said Pat.

"No, this is definitely our last summer," Kevin replied. "We're lucky to still be around."

"Angelo died last year and he wasn't even as bad off as we are."

"We'll die in the winter. It's always in winter. I've heard that you can die just from a cold."

"Heaven. Kevin, what's it like?"

"You're with Jesus all the time," Kevin said with conviction.

"No one is sick," Pat continued. "And you can walk, everyone can walk."

"Pat, you can run. Even if you never could run before."

I never discussed mortality with Kevin and Pat. At twenty-one, I would not have known what to say to those two seventeen-year-olds who, despite their age, had more insight into death than most adults. I doubt their parents discussed it very much either.

Where could you begin? But that night I heard them talk matter-of-factly about their own deaths. They sounded scared, but also hopeful and resolved. I think they both felt lucky to have someone to talk to, someone who would understand their hopes and fears completely. I admired them for their courage, and I was glad that neither of them had to contemplate death alone.

Pat died that winter, and Kevin the winter after that. If there is any order or sense to the universe, they are running together right now, children who lived and died with love and nobility.

In the summer of 1973, I was a third-year medical student finishing up my first month on the wards at Boston City Hospital. It was a period when I was constantly learning, putting all the lessons from the classroom into practice at the bedside. The basics of taking a personal history and conducting a physical exam were coming along fine, but the complexities of patient care were still formidable. On a very foggy day in July, I was doing clinical rounds with my attending when an emergency alert was announced over the loudspeakers.

We had done emergency drills before. When the alarm went off, we would congregate in designated areas and review the steps we would take in an actual emergency, sometimes even simulating the response and having nonessential personnel leave the building. The drills were meant to be as realistic as possible, but someone always knew about them ahead of time. A nurse would warn you not to put your lunch in the microwave, since we were about to head downstairs for a drill and that leftover pasta would be cold by the time we got back.

But today, no one had warned us of a drill. Every available pair of hands in Boston City Hospital was summoned to the Accident Floor of the emergency center, which was chaotic with activity.

Stretchers were being lined up, and busy nurses and physicians were laying out all the materials for dressing wounds, starting IVs, and beginning blood transfusions. Everything was prepared for resuscitation: every room on the ward was being equipped with a defibrillator, the machine that jolts patients with an electric shock to restart their heart during cardiac arrest. Everyone was there: students, residents, radiologists, pediatricians—whoever was available to help in what appeared to be the preparations for a mass casualty event. This was not a drill. Only war, I thought, could require such massive teams ready for an undefined emergency.

I did not know what was coming, but I took account of what I could do. Yes, chest compressions, mouth to mouth, and starting intravenous lines. But I still did not feel comfortable inserting a breathing tube, and I had never actually identified and responded to the various heartbeat abnormalities that could occur in an emergency and which I had studied in my textbooks. But whatever was coming, I was resolved to stay completely calm and contribute in any way that I could. I was proud and willing to play a part in the lifesaving work that was clearly going to be required of us.

But as quickly as the emergency was called, it was over. "You can all leave now," someone announced. People began to disperse, some convinced that this was just a very thorough drill. But a few nurses had tears in their eyes, and others were quietly discussing the news they had just received.

That morning, Delta Air Lines Flight 723 from Manchester, New Hampshire was attempting to land at Boston's Logan International Airport. Upon its approach, the runway was obscured by heavy fog. The flight crew asked for assistance, but ground control was distracted by a potential collision between two other planes. Poorly positioned, the pilot attempted to land, but the plane went off course and crashed into a seawall three thousand feet short of the runway. Upon contact, the plane split apart, spewing passengers and burning fuel along the runway.

Immediately, emergency preparedness teams had gone to work at Boston City Hospital and Massachusetts General. We had been called upon to use every resource we had to save the lives of the men, women, and children who were on that flight. We were ready to stop bleeding, set bones, and dress wounds. We were ready to pump air into failing lungs and shock hearts back to life. But on that morning in late July, eighty-two passengers and six crew members died at the scene of the crash. An army sergeant who had managed to escape the broken burning plane was transferred to a burn unit at Massachusetts General. The lone survivor of the crash, he died in the hospital four months later.

Leaving work that day, I contemplated the massive tragedy. I thought about our frantic, futile work, our vain efforts to stop pain, suffering, and death. My mind turned from the victims that we did not have the opportunity to save to the families they left behind. These were victims I felt equally powerless to help. I tried to imagine their sudden, violent grief. I could barely fathom their shock, anger, and despair. There is no morphine for that type of pain, and my heart ached at the thought of losing someone I loved so suddenly and forever.

At around 9:00 a.m. on January 18, 1977, a forty-eight-year-old man was brought to the Accident Floor of Boston City Hospital, quite literally frozen to death. Ambulance drivers had found him comatose in the hallway of an abandoned apartment building. Apparently he had fallen asleep after a heavy night of drinking and spent nearly twelve hours exposed to below-freezing temperatures in the unheated building. When he came in, his skin was cold. Pulse, blood pressure, breathing, and heart sounds of any kind were all completely undetectable. His pupils were dilated, and he did not respond to any stimuli. His body temperature was about 75 degrees Fahrenheit, twenty-three degrees below normal. Essentially he was dead, and in most hospitals he would have been declared so on the spot.

But the Boston City residents were a very aggressive group, and they began cardiopulmonary resuscitation—CPR. Such resuscitation starts simply: chest compression and assisted breathing through a tight-fitting mask and a bag that squeezes air into the lungs. The patient received continuous CPR for an hour. With the mask providing 100 percent oxygen to his lungs, physicians and nurses took turns keeping up sixty to one hundred chest compressions per minute. Performing effective CPR is a physically taxing job. You must use both hands and all your body weight to compress the chest hard enough to squeeze the heart. This artificially keeps the heart pumping and blood circulating throughout the body. If oxygen stops flowing to the brain and vital organs, the body will completely shut down.

The scene surrounding the frozen patient was controlled chaos, with the senior medicine resident giving all the orders. Equipment seemed to appear spontaneously: an intravenous line to pump warm fluids into his body and bring up his temperature; an EKG machine to search for his heartbeat; a Foley catheter to monitor urination; and an endotracheal tube to simulate breathing. There were perhaps a dozen nurses, physicians, and X-ray technicians each with a specific role to perform. After a full hour of frenzied activity, the patient's EKG was still flat: no heartbeat. After two hours, he was still lying motionless on the stretcher.

However, at 11:55 a.m., a trace heartbeat was detected and the patient began to revive. Excitement and optimism permeated the crowded room. Nowhere else would CPR have been continued for so long on a patient with no heartbeat. But the team had recognized that this man was essentially frozen in time. The freezing temperatures that killed him also preserved him for this heroic resuscitation. He had been dead for hours, and now he was alive.

Late in the afternoon, the patient was transferred from the emergency room to the intensive care unit, where his condition was stabilized and he began his long road to full recovery. While he was frozen, the man's kidneys had shut down and he had developed pneumonia, internal bleeding, and heart failure. He was in the hospital for over a month, and during that time every resident in the program participated in some aspect of his care. His story was well known throughout the hospital, and everyone had taken to calling him "the Iceman."

I was working night shifts in the ICU at the time. I monitored his blood sugar and regulated his insulin doses. Eventually, his regimen became routine, but each time I saw the Iceman, I continued to marvel at his case. He had been practically dead for hours, but five weeks later, mild diabetes was once again his biggest health concern.

When he fully recovered, the Iceman walked out of Boston City Hospital on his own, with no signs of brain damage. He was awake, alert, and content. We were all proud of the role, large or small, that we each played in his miraculous recovery. There was a celebration of sorts as he left the hospital and started life anew. All of the physicians and nurses who had taken part in his care saw him off with balloons and a tray of cookies. I never heard what happened to him after that. Hopefully he is alive and well, and somewhere warm. Obviously, on that winter night in Boston, his time had not come.

His was one of the longest successful resuscitations ever performed, and it helped change the thinking on how patients with such low body temperature should be handled. His story revealed that we simply do not know the real limits of nature and the human body. We cannot predict who will fall and who will be pulled back from the brink, who will cross and perhaps recross the thin line that separates life and death.

In 1990, I was the chairman of the Department of Medicine at ETSU, and administrative duties were taking up more and more of my time. I still saw patients, however, and in June a patient named Eric came to see me because he was having trouble sleeping. About one year prior to the visit, Eric had been in a bad motorcycle accident in California. He survived the collision and was taken to the emergency room, where they treated his injuries and gave him a blood transfusion to replace the blood he had lost. Several months later, Eric's injuries were healing, but his doctors could not explain his persistent fatigue and poor health. Eric was married and had a young daughter; he did not fit the profile of someone at risk for HIV and AIDS. His doctors finally made the diagnosis (the virus had been transmitted through the blood transfusion he got after his accident), but by that time he was in the later stages of the disease.

In the late eighties, there was only one drug available to treat AIDS: AZT. When Eric had a bad reaction to the drug, he was told there was no hope and that he had six months to live. He took all of his savings—$30,000—and went on vacation in Europe with his wife and daughter. When the money ran out, he moved his family from California to a small town outside of Johnson City where his in-laws lived. I was the new physician Eric came to see when he moved.

The first time I saw Eric, he was in decent but failing health. He was very thin but still looked handsome and even youthful, wearing a white shirt and white pants. I found out later that his preference for white was a vestige of his years as a chef. His skin was pale, but not jaundiced, and there was one small raised purple bump on his forehead, a telltale sign of progressive AIDS. When I asked him how he was coping with his diagnosis, he spoke in a relaxed tone, relaxed as most who have resigned themselves to death. It was clear that, for him, this visit was routine and perhaps even futile and unimportant.

"I'm still sad sometimes," he replied. "I used to ask myself, Why me? I'm not gay and I don't use drugs. But I've gotten over that. I've learned to accept what happened. I still want to see my little girl grow up, but I realize that I could have easily died from my bike accident. I'm glad I got the chance to plan the time I have left."

Eric told me that he had come in that day to get help with his insomnia, that he just wanted a prescription for a sleep aid that would get him through the nights. However, I wanted to discuss something else.

"Your visit today is not just about sleeping pills," I told him. "Eric, there are new drugs that have been developed just in the last few months. We shouldn't look at your diagnosis as a death sentence. I think we should keep searching for new treatment options." I did not know whether Eric wanted sleeping pills for insomnia or for something else, but I could tell that he had stopped looking to the future. I wanted to restore his hope and his desire to fight for survival. I was careful not to overstate the new advances, but I wanted to tell him that he might still see his little girl grow up.

He was cautious. Like so many AIDS patients at that time, he had come to accept his own death as impending and inevitable. I respected and admired him for the dignity with which he faced the prospect of death, but I also strongly believed that death was not so near as he thought it was. I was glad when he agreed to reconsider treatment and stopped pursuing a prescription for sleeping pills.

As it turns out, Eric was not even allergic to AZT but to a sulfa medicine that he had taken at the same time. We put him on a powerful three-drug regimen, and his status improved. His CD4 count, a measure of the health of the immune system, went from zero to normal level. Had the disease gone untreated for another few months, Eric's death would indeed have been as predicted. But he remained among the living, becoming strong and reestablishing dreams for himself and his wife and daughter. He opened a restaurant. I regret that I never acted on his invitation to visit.

As an infectious disease specialist in the 1980s and 1990s, I saw HIV/AIDS transform in the social consciousness from a stigmatized, shameful disease into a legitimate and important health concern. In the field of medicine, the virus went from being seen as an agonizing death sentence to a manageable chronic illness. I bore witness to deaths that were painful, but dignified, and I saw patients who fought nobly and vigorously for their survival. Most importantly, however, I saw hope turn dying men like Eric into fighters. I learned that hope can be more powerful than fear, more important than courage, and more potent than a drug in the face of death.

• • •

As an attending physician at East Tennessee State University College of Medicine, I would see each new admission to the hospital with several students and junior residents in tow. I had to make sure that my patients got excellent care while my students got hands-on learning experience. Sometimes striking this balance was difficult, but there was one resident who made my job easier. Dr. Tom Ronald had graduated from the University of South Carolina School of Medicine but came back to his hometown of Johnson City for residency.

On rounds with me, Tom learned the basics of listening to patients and examining them. He was an average resident in ability but extraordinary in enthusiasm. He was a natural caregiver, and he loved his interactions with patients. He enjoyed patiently and carefully listening to each individual history, making a diagnosis, and choosing a suitable treatment. I can still picture him at the bedside of his patients. He had brownish red hair, blue eyes, and a ruddy complexion. He seemed to smile with reluctance and had the habit of looking up in the air when he couldn't find the right words to say.

Just prior to beginning his residency, Tom had been diagnosed with melanoma, an aggressive skin cancer. The cancer was already in the progressive stages of malignancy, and his prognosis was not good. Nevertheless, he went forward with his residency, and only asked that his fellow residents not be told about his illness. Tom wanted to be appreciated as an intern, not as a person with cancer. He aspired to be a professor and medical school attending himself, someday. Though he bore the scar of a biopsy on his neck above the collar, no one knew about his diagnosis and no one ever asked.

Tom made tremendous progress during his first year of residency, but unfortunately so did his cancer. He began walking slowly through the hallways of the hospital, and sometimes I noticed a slight limp and a grimace of pain that would leave his face the moment he entered a patient's room. Toward the end of the year, Tom had a seizure, and an MRI confirmed that the cancer had spread to his brain. After that, his health declined rapidly. He suffered repeated seizures, a humeral fracture, intracranial surgery, and radiation to the spine. Throughout the debilitating treatments, Tom continued to express his unhampered desire to return to the wards and move on to his second year of residency. He worked hard to regain his strength and mobility, despite the aggressive nature of his cancer and its treatments, both of which continued to do damage to his body.

About three months after his first seizure, Tom's condition improved slightly, and he was well enough to join my team on attending rounds. He was more outgoing and inquisitive than I had ever seen him. His back hurt him, and he would later describe how formidable the long hallways had been, but he was delighted and exhilarated that he was once again participating in patient care. He made plans to return the next week, but his condition quickly deteriorated as the tumor in his brain grew even more rapidly than anyone could have predicted. Tom returned to the hospital the next week, but this time as a patient.

Within days of his admission, I was at Tom's bedside at Johnson City Medical Center with a team of his fellow residents. He was in and out of consciousness, but on two occasions he inquired about the meningitis patient he had been following. He apologized for missing rounds.

"We all missed you, but you will be back with us soon. Tom, I want you to know that we are all proud of you."

He smiled. He knew that he had been a great success.

I stood at his bedside and watched him die just an hour later. I cried when I spoke to his parents. I told them how grateful and proud I was to have been a part of Tom's life and his education. I let them know how sorry I was to lose such a wonderful person and physician.

It was difficult for me to make sense of the tragedy that had befallen us. The job of a physician is to fight against disease, suffering, and death in others; it is shocking and incomprehensible when we lose one of our own. The morning after Tom's death, I addressed the seventy-five residents who had been his colleagues. "Everyone who knew Tom will want his death to have some enduring meaning. For me, in those moments when teaching seems mundane, when I ask myself how many years I can teach and say the same thing with undissipated enthusiasm, when I wonder if anyone cares in the age of a disturbed health care system, I will make-believe that I am at Tom's last rounds and will do my best. I wish there is more that I could do."

I was a pallbearer at Tom's funeral; the others were fellow residents, who returned to the hospital promptly after the burial. That was fitting. Tom wanted to spend every moment he had at the bedside of a patient who needed him, and he would not have wanted to keep his colleagues from doing the same. Then and now, I try to see beyond the tragedy of Tom's death, to the lesson of his life, which taught us about true selflessness in the medical profession.

In April of 1995, my mother called me from Florida. From her voice, I could immediately tell that she was troubled, and when I asked what was bothering her, she told me that my dad had been staring at his income tax return data for the entire day. Dad was excellent at math, having been a chemistry major and a businessman. He filled out their tax return every year without difficulty, but that day he could not complete a single form. When I spoke with him, he had trouble explaining the situation, but the next day when I checked in, he was back to feeling normal and had made progress on his taxes.

We thought that Dad was just having a bad day, but in retrospect we saw it was the first sign of Alzheimer's, a degenerative disease that afflicts the elderly and causes progressive dementia, debilitation, and ultimately death. When my dad was diagnosed, I was already extremely familiar with the disease and its effects on both patients and families. In addition to my training in infectious disease, I had also subspecialized in geriatrics. In Johnson City, I organized and spoke at a congressional hearing on Alzheimer's disease on the Veterans Administration campus. In Amarillo, I set up the Alzheimer's Academy, a program where geriatricians met with family members to advise them on how to cope with the disease and best guide their loved ones through the incredible challenges at every stage. For example, the decision to take away car keys from an Alzheimer's patient is always difficult. One West Texas family from a town of two hundred told us that their dad could no longer drive safely, but it was okay. Everyone in town knew his car, and they would get off the road when they saw him coming.

Every course of Alzheimer's is different, and in my dad's case the progression was very slow. Within a year or two, we began to worry about his driving. He also lost the ability to tell time, and he began to have trouble following or participating in conversations. Eventually, he became so quiet that he would prefer not to speak to anyone but family. Always an avid reader, he now spent a lot of time reading news periodicals and magazines (his memory got too weak for him to keep up with the long novels he used to love). In many cases, Alzheimer's can cause so much neuronal damage in the brain that it will change a patient's personality. But we were fortunate. Throughout the challenges of his progressive dementia, Dad maintained the patient, kind, and gentle disposition he had throughout his life. He would not lose his temper, say an angry word, or make an unkind remark, and enjoyed spending quiet time with his wife and family.

By 2000 we decided that Dad would be better off if he were closer to us. He was in good spirits, but his health was declining and he needed my help and support. The move from Delray Beach to Amarillo was difficult for my mom, but my dad was glad to be able to see me every day when I dropped by after work. Jeremy called them all the time from college, and Justin was a frequent visitor to their house. For the most part, Mom and Dad took care of themselves when they first moved, but it was a comfort to know I would be available to help them if anything ever happened. In the end, I think we were all glad to have family close by.

In Amarillo, Dad's primary physician was Dr. Steve Urban, the most distinguished internist in the community. Rather than using the standard mental status exam to assess the effectiveness of a medication regimen, Dr. Urban would ask his patients about something they were familiar with or interested in. He knew Dad was from New York and a Yankees fan, so Dr. Urban always asked about the team at every visit. Before every one of his appointments, Dad would study the box scores and standings in the newspaper, preparing for his quiz.

Inevitably, despite a good response to available medication, Dad became more confused. When there was something important, such as a trip or doctor's appointment the next day, he would get up and dress in the wee hours of the morning. He was aware of his condition getting worse. Once he told me that he just felt like he was no longer all there—he estimated that his brain was half of what it had been. But he also told me that he had lived life fully, enjoyed a long and wonderful retirement, traveled everywhere, and played tennis each day for more than ten years. He insisted that he was ready to go when the time came and said it would make no sense to just stay alive when he could no longer think right. Dad was always very consistent when making decisions about the type of life-extending medical care he would pursue. In 2001 he was diagnosed with mild kidney disease and decided not to undergo dialysis. I was not surprised, therefore, when he told me explicitly that he did not want his body to be kept alive in a hospital if his mind had already gone before.

In late March 2005, I got another troubled phone call from my mother. Dad had fallen while trying to go to the bathroom. When he tried to get up, he fell again and could not move. I rushed to their home, but I knew before I got there that he had broken his hip. As a geriatrician, I had frequently taught about hip fractures as a prelude to the downhill course of an octogenarian, particularly one with Alzheimer's disease. Some patients do not survive the surgery to reconstruct a broken hip, but Dad pulled through. While he was recovering in the hospital, we devised a call schedule to watch over him at night, since he would not call the nurses to help him use the urinal or adjust positions. A senior in high school, Justin frequently cared for him on the weekends, reading in a chair by his bed all night long. It reminded me of the time when Justin got pneumonia as a toddler, and Dad stayed up with him for two nights in a row, holding him in a sitting position because it was easier to breathe when upright.

After being discharged from the hospital, Dad worked hard on recovering at the overnight rehab unit near his home. It was heartbreaking to see him struggle in the unfamiliar environment.

With his disorientation in time and space, poor hearing, and general inability to understand directions, he would panic whenever my mom left his side, even for a moment. He particularly hated being left alone in a crowded room, surrounded by strangers. I think he was glad to leave the rehab center.

When he came back home, Dad became quiet, frustrated, and even irritable on occasion. In May 2006, I was on the road from Amarillo to Lubbock for Texas Tech's medical school graduation. I got a phone call that my father was experiencing some abdominal pain and that he had filled the commode with blood and black stool. His blood pressure had dropped, and it was clear that he was having gastrointestinal bleeding. I changed direction on Interstate 27 and returned home immediately.

Internal bleeding was a sign that my dad was nearing the end, and it would have been ample cause to seek hospitalization. However, Dad had already indicated that he did not want to die in a hospital, that he preferred to die at home with family members nearby. I was not sure of what to do, and I did my best to find out what he wanted.

I tried to explain the situation. I said, "Dad, you will not make it here at home. We can go to the hospital and they will give you blood and IVs, or we can stay here at home. But if we stay here, you just won't make it—I think you would die here." At first he seemed confused and surprised because I had always, always presented an optimistic view of his health. But this time I needed him to understand the options.

He consoled me, telling me not to be so upset, that this was his time. He was eighty-six. He said that my mom would be okay in Amarillo. We did not take him to the hospital, and I expected him to die that night. But death is not so predictable.

He survived at home for twenty days. I was at his bedside every day and every night for nearly three weeks. I worked with hospice and dispensed morphine for his periods of pain and agitation or to control his rapid breathing. He went in and out of coma; at times he became very still and seemed close to the end, but he would briefly awake, even smile, as if not quite ready to die. But there did come a day when his breathing became agonized and infrequent. I knew it was finally the end. I watched the very last gasp for breath and realized that the thin line separating life from death had disappeared. The trade-off was made: peace, the end of suffering, cognitive decline, and disability, but in exchange for an eternity without his unique smile—his words of advice, experience, and wisdom lost forever. Dad had said his good-byes as best he could and even chose, to an extent, his time and place.

Fourteen months before my father's death, I am contemplating my own death in the driver's seat of a stranger's car.

"I'm going to kill you right here."

I do not want to die here, out behind my house, in a stranger's car, by a stranger's gun. At age fifty-five, perhaps I have lived longer than the great majority of men born to this earth. Perhaps I have accomplished more than any person should hope for or expect. But I do not want to die. My wife has just come home from church, and my son is waiting for me to help him with his term paper.

"Open the door." His voice is insistent and threatening.

Don't panic. I find the garage door opener on the floor with my foot. I bend down, pick it up, and open the garage door. *I am spared for now. I will survive this ordeal.*

The garage door opens slowly, and we see my wife's green minivan parked in the middle spot. I take a deep breath. It is time for negotiation.

"I will do whatever you want, but stay in the garage and don't come through the door," I ask calmly. Unexpectedly, he agrees. He just wants cash, and I believe he asks for jewelry, though it's possible that the jewelry was my suggestion. He wants it to happen quickly, though, so I promise him, swear to him that I will return soon. "Just don't come in the house." He agrees. He does not want to meet my wife. He tells me that he will let me go as soon as I bring him what he asks for. I expect to be released right down the street and believe that my ordeal is close to its end.

I enter my home without him.

State of Texas v. Jack Lindsey Jordan

> DEFENSE ATTORNEY BAILEY: You made the comment that you were arguing or pleading with Mr. Jordan about going back to the house. Can you explain what you were talking about?
>
> STEVEN BERK: I didn't want to go back to the house because my wife would be there.
>
> BAILEY: Were you arguing or pleading, or was there a difference?
>
> BERK: I guess he had the gun. It was more pleading.
>
> BAILEY: Now in regard to actually going back to your home, was there a gentleman's agreement between the two of you?
>
> BERK: Kind of.
>
> BAILEY: And that conversation was that you would only be in the house for sixty seconds?
>
> BERK: He may have just said to get in and get out.
>
> . . .

DISTRICT ATTORNEY BLOUNT: Was there a conversation between you and Dr. Berk regarding you going into the house?

JACK LINDSEY JORDAN: Yes sir.

BLOUNT: And what was that conversation?

JORDAN: That I wouldn't go into the house because I didn't want to meet his wife.

5

Aequanimitas

I met Shirley in 1979, shortly after moving to Tennessee from Boston. She was a microbiologist, and I was the only infectious disease physician in eastern Tennessee; so our professional paths crossed frequently. She would call me to ask for my opinion on an unusual culture or to identify an unfamiliar strain of bacteria. Eventually, I was visiting the microbiology lab multiple times a day. Later, I would joke that she called me to the lab so often that I had to marry her, just to get any work done.

Shirley was born and raised in East Tennessee, and when I met her, she had never been out of the area. She was a Republican from the rural South, and I considered myself a liberal from the urban North. Considering our different backgrounds and upbringings, perhaps it was an unlikely match. But thirty years of marriage have proven that we are well suited to share both our lives and our careers.

In our early years together in Tennessee we studied the causes of pneumonia. I was working at the Veterans Administration

Hospital, and pneumonia was a major concern for the older patients I saw there. At that time, the different bacteria that cause pneumonia in the elderly were not well known or understood. Through careful collection methods and culture techniques, Shirley and I were finding bacteria that were not yet appreciated as causes of pneumonia. We published many papers on the subject, and our work led to a better understanding of the disease, particularly in older populations. Years later, after we had children, Shirley and I once boasted at the dinner table that we had discovered a new cause of pneumonia. The next week, we received a call from Justin's preschool teacher, who was excited to have us come to class and bring the new type of *ammonia* we'd discovered. He had told her we were scientists when she asked the class what their parents did for a living.

After our sons were born, Shirley continued to work part-time in microbiology. This also allowed her time to dedicate herself to different causes in our community. In 1997 she was elected to the Johnson City Board of Education, and in 1999 she was elected as its vice chairman. Shirley was responsible for important reforms during her term on the board. Her support of redistricting to give racial minorities fairer representation was not popular with some of our physician friends, but it was an issue that she believed in and did not back down from. Her efforts on that front were consistent with her character. Shirley has a strong, innate impulse to fight for the underdog, and for as long as I have known her, she has worked quietly and selflessly to improve the lives of everyone around her.

I have always been impressed with Shirley's generosity. When we were still in East Tennessee, I served for many years as the faculty adviser to the Student National Medical Association, and her support of the students we met through that program was unmatched. The SNMA is an organization for minority medical students, which aims to address the unique needs and concerns that students of color face in the medical profession. In Johnson City, most minority students did not come from East Tennessee, but from Nashville or Memphis. They were far from home and often without a strong support network. Shirley and I both felt strongly about our involvement with the program. We hosted many events at our home, including the annual Christmas party. Shirley got to know the students personally, and she helped many of them get summer jobs in the microbiology lab at ETSU. If students were ever in particular need, Shirley never failed to loan them the money they needed to pay for a trip home, a ticket to an interview, or the tuition for a board review course. Shirley would write them a check and tell them not to mention it again.

Shirley has a knack for taking care of other people. In our family, she is the glue that holds us all together. For the boys, and often for me, Shirley is the best source of important information, support, and advice. I did not even know my own PIN number because my wife is so diligent and capable when it comes to managing our household and finances. Jeremy and Justin seek out Shirley's expertise on subjects large and small. Whether they have forgotten the price of stamps or their own pant size, whether they need her advice about planning flights home or applying for a job, the boys are never disappointed when they call their mother. Shirley always has the answer. Without Shirley, no part of our family life would function smoothly.

In addition to being kind and generous, Shirley is completely fearless. I have never seen her frightened by anything. When she gave birth to our boys, she required no reassurance or comforting. She did not complain and expressed only mild annoyance when I tried to use the Lamaze skills I had learned to prepare for the event. I think her Tennessee background is partly responsible for Shirley's fearlessness. When I first met her, she was living alone in a house that she owned, somewhat on the outskirts of town. I once asked her if she ever felt nervous as a single woman in a fairly deserted area, and she simply replied, "I have a gun, and I know how to use it."

I was a bit surprised by her answer. She was the first person I had ever known who owned a gun, but perhaps I should have expected it. Tennessee has a culture of gun ownership. Shirley's father was a hunter who owned many guns, displaying them proudly in a special cabinet at home, and Shirley had taken shooting lessons when she was younger. At county fairs and shooting galleries, the boys and I were always impressed with her marksmanship.

Throughout our married life in Tennessee, we kept Shirley's gun in a high cabinet in the kitchen. She always told me that if she were robbed or confronted by an intruder, she would not hesitate to shoot him. That was the philosophy of East Tennessee as well as West Texas. When the doorbell rang late at night, she might take the gun with her to answer it.

"And Steve, if you ever shoot someone and they make it out of your house, don't leave them out on the lawn. Drag them back into the house. That is what law enforcement would want to see." I was shocked by that statement. When I would try to joke about it with my neighbors, however, they would just nod as if to say, "Of course. Good advice."

When we moved to Texas, Shirley decided not to bring the gun with us. The kids were getting older, and, unlike Shirley, they had never handled a gun or learned how to use one. Plus, in all the years she owned a gun, Shirley had never needed it. The only crime she had ever been a victim of was when her hubcaps were stolen during a friend's wedding in Chattanooga. So before we moved to Amarillo, Shirley decided that having a gun in the house was not worth the risk. I agreed, and so we left her hand-gun in Johnson City.

I don't know how things would have turned out on the day of my kidnapping if we had kept a gun. Perhaps I would have gone into the house and come back with a weapon to drive away the intruder who was waiting for me in the garage. Perhaps I would have gunned him down right there in my garage, or gotten killed myself.

When I entered our house that day, there was no gun inside, just Shirley at the kitchen counter preparing lunch. Even without a gun, I had options at that point. I could have called the police, or run with Shirley out the front door of our house to a neigh-bor's. I could have gathered up all the cash and valuables in the house and gone back to the garage, telling my wife on my way out to call the police. There were plenty of options, but I had only one goal at that point: keep my family safe. I did not want Shirley to be involved at all. I did not want her to know that the man in our garage even existed. I had kept Justin safe by staying calm and acting like nothing was wrong. I would do the same with Shirley. I would deal with this event in the only way I knew how: with aequanimitas.

Sir William Osler was born in 1849 and died in 1919. He is per-haps the best-known physician of the twentieth century. I have always taken great interest in the history of medicine, and I have always found Osler particularly fascinating. I consider myself an Osler scholar, and throughout my career I have written exten-sively about the physician and what he stood for. I am a member of the American Osler Society, a group committed to remembering and honoring the man and his teachings. Osler was the ideal practitioner: a humanist, a physician, and a philosopher. He wrote eloquently about the practice of medicine and the qualities essential to being a good physician. He transformed medical education in the United States when he became chairman of medicine at Johns Hopkins.

Osler had deep insight into the fundamentals of practicing medicine. He taught about the importance of the careful physical examination, and wrote about how various findings from a physical examination could be used in diagnosis. He emphasized the importance of the most basic bedside skill: carefully listening to patients about their complaints. This is important not only as a way of developing the proper physician-patient relationship but of learning the facts about the medical problem so that the right diagnosis can be made. Today, many physicians rely too much on expensive lab tests and diagnostic technology, and forget the fundamental value of a close physical examination. For this reason, Osler's teachings are still vital and relevant today.

But Osler taught another enduring lesson that has had a deep impact on my own life, both before and since my kidnapping. Osler advised about the personal qualities that must be developed in young physicians. Of all the characteristics Osler felt a doctor should embody, there was none more important to him than "aequanimitas."

He wrote:

> In the physician or surgeon no quality takes rank with imperturbability. . . . Imperturbability means coolness and presence of mind under all circumstances, calmness amid storm, and clearness of judgment in moments of great peril, immobility, impassiveness. It is the quality which is

most appreciated by the laity though often misunderstood by them.

Aequanimitas is indissolubly associated with wide experience and intimate knowledge of the varied aspects of disease. With such advantages the physician is so equipped that no eventuality can disturb his mental equilibrium; the possibilities are always manifest and the course of action clear.[1]

The practice of medicine is intimately wound up in the most emotionally charged moments of life and death. At times, it can be chaotic, stressful, and dramatic, and the only way to perform under such conditions is to remain composed and rational, and often emotionally detached from situations that call for controlled, decisive action. Throughout my career as a doctor, developing and maintaining aequanimitas has been one of my greatest challenges. I have been called upon many times to act skillfully under pressure, and these have been some of the most memorable and educational experiences in my career.

Before my residency, when I was still in my third year at Boston University, I did an internal medicine rotation at Boston City Hospital. On the very first day of that three-month rotation, I was met by a very busy intern who needed assistance.

"Hey, can you put down an NG [nasogastric] tube?"

He was holding several charts, and his white coat pockets were overflowing with papers and blood-filled tubes that needed to be taken to the laboratory. His fingertips were dyed blue from the stains we used to view bacteria on microscope slides. His eyes were a bit glazed. One could always tell who had been on call the night before, who was completing their thirty-six-hour shift.

"Well, I've never done one," I replied.

"Seen one done?" he asked, still hopeful.

"Yes, one." (Actually, two, if you included the time our professor put one into his own stomach during our basic physiology class in the first year of medical school.)

"Well, you know it's pretty easy. When you put the tube down the nose, there's nowhere else it can go but into the stomach. Just put enough jelly on the end of it."

"Well, I guess I can do it."

"Okay, room 234."

I went down the hall to the room of a pleasant older man who did not speak much. I explained the procedure. In my hands, I held a narrow flexible plastic tube, a small packet of K-Y jelly, and suction hookup. I was almost ready to begin when a jolly, middle-aged nurse stuck her head into the room.

"Oh! Are you putting an NG tube down?"

"I think so . . . Yes, I am. I'm putting down an NG tube." I felt uneasy about admitting to the deed, as if I was an imposter who would soon be arrested for impersonating a real doctor. *Why does she ask?* I wondered.

"Well, just wait for one more minute," she said.

After several minutes, she returned followed by several nurses. *Oh God,* I thought, *she's brought more witnesses.* On closer inspection, however, the nurses were actually nursing students, looking young, fresh, curious, and very neat in their uniforms. They surrounded me and the patient in a semicircle, spaced equally apart.

"Now could you explain what you're doing, step by step?" asked the jolly nurse.

"Well, of course." I took a deep breath and tried to stay calm.

Now I will impersonate both an intern and a professor of nursing. I began the procedure, narrating my progress. I managed to open the little package of jelly. *Great, step one down.* I put jelly on the end of the tube and leaned the patient's head back. I pointed the tube toward the back of the nose and asked the patient to swallow. There was some resistance, but the tube disappeared down his throat somewhere. I said something about how well the procedure was going.

The tube went down, and the students were pleased. I had completed my first great labor in the medical profession. Like a master surgeon, I performed the procedure with grace and effectiveness. Osler would have been glad to see a medical student learn by doing, practicing both the skill and the composure that are required of all physicians. That was the first time I got through an unfamiliar or difficult patient encounter by taking things one step at a time, but it was by no means the last.

For many years Dr. J. K. Smith was my supervisor at ETSU in Johnson City. He was my department chairman and a brilliant clinician and teacher. Professionally, we shared many interests, including the study of pneumonia, and we always had a collegial relationship.

In fact, I can remember only one instance of professional tension with JK. He had been asked by a young resident to see a very ill older man who was in the hospital for pneumonia. The patient had been prescribed various antibiotics, but the infection had not responded to any of them. The man had refused ventilator support, and his condition was quickly deteriorating. The resident managing his case wanted to identify the organism that was causing the pneumonia, hoping that determining the cause of infection would lead to a more suitable treatment.

After examining the patient, Dr. Smith told the resident to call me to do a transtracheal aspirate procedure. This was a method once commonly used to determine the cause of pneumonia. It involves puncturing a small membrane in the neck above the trachea called the cricothyroid membrane. A catheter is inserted through the puncture site and threaded down the trachea, which connects to the lungs. Inserting the catheter irritates the airways and causes the patient to cough, bringing up infected material from the lungs, through the catheter, and into a syringe, where it is collected and analyzed to determine what strain of bacteria is causing the infection.

I had performed transtracheal aspirate procedures routinely, both in Boston and in Tennessee. However, this patient had a condition that made the procedure extremely dangerous to perform. He suffered from a severe bleeding problem called disseminated intravascular coagulation (DIC), a disorder that made him particularly prone to uncontrolled bleeding in response to any type of trauma. I knew that even a small mistake in pointing the catheter needle might result in severe bleeding. Puncturing the thyroid gland or accidentally nicking open a vein could cause massive damage and blood loss. The patient's DIC was a total contraindication to performing the procedure, and when the resident asked me to do it on behalf of Dr. Smith, I refused.

However, later that day, I got another call from the same resident, who was embarrassed to be in the middle of a disagreement between the department chairman and the chief of infectious disease. "Dr. Berk, he told me to tell you to do it!"

JK was not available for further discussion.

I do not typically take risks with patients; I do not have that mentality. But a respected colleague had made a decision about a patient who needed help, and so, against my better judgment, I acquiesced. Despite my doubts, I knew that I had to stay calm and confident throughout the procedure.

When I arrived, the patient was lying on the examining table, wide awake. I was wearing a gown and gloves to maintain sterile conditions around the incision I was about to make. To prepare the site, I painted the patient's neck in an orange solution of betadine, an antiseptic. Using a small needle, I delivered a small dose of local anesthetic to the area of his neck just above the membrane. Then I used a scalpel to make a tiny nick in his skin where the needle and then the catheter would be inserted into his trachea. There was a bit more superficial bleeding than I was used to, but I went ahead and inserted the catheter needle through the cricothyroid membrane. The patient began to cough immediately, and the tube was instantly filled with thick, green, infected mucus from his lungs. Blood oozed from the site of insertion, and I began to worry about his bleeding. *Apply direct pressure; hope there are no punctures in his trachea.* The patient continued to cough, but despite bleeding around the incision, there was no blood in the mucus. The catheter had gone down smoothly, and we were able to obtain the infected material that held the key to finding an effective treatment.

The mucus was sent to the lab, where the technician discovered that it was full of staphylococcus bacteria. Certain strains of staph are known to be highly resistant to most antibiotics, and today it can be very difficult to treat a staph infection. However, at the time we still had a good alternative antibiotic that usually worked against the bacteria: vancomycin. The patient received a full round of the drug, and his condition steadily improved. In the end, JK was right, and the procedure led to a good outcome. Though I had been proven wrong, I was able to keep my composure throughout. I did not let pride or fear stand in the way of doing my job well. I stayed calm while performing a risky procedure that ultimately led to positive results.

. . .

Bobby was my patient for several years while I was still at ETSU in Johnson City. He was quiet, polite, and thoughtful, and looked almost boyish at the age of twenty. Blonde with fair skin, he gave the impression of great vulnerability. Bobby was diagnosed with AIDS at the age of nineteen, and he was my patient from the beginning. He would come in for regular appointments to monitor his CD4 count and keep an eye on signs of infection or decline. Every time he came in, he was accompanied by his boyfriend, John, and they appeared to have a very stable and caring relationship. In 1996, despite a year of being HIV positive, Bobby had not had any serious complications, and John had remained HIV negative.

In fact, the biggest challenge Bobby had faced since his diagnosis had not been medical at all. When Bobby had informed his family that he had AIDS and that he was gay and living with a very close boyfriend, his parents had been traumatized and practically disowned him. In East Tennessee at that time, such a revelation was overwhelming, even for Bobby's close-knit family. He had not spoken with his parents in nearly a year.

That June, however, Bobby took a vacation with his parents to Florida. It was a trip he had been looking forward to, and I was hopeful that it would be good for everyone involved. Sadly, upon his return, Bobby was in very poor condition. He was admitted to the emergency room following a dramatic change in his mental status. Bobby's parents reported that he had suffered from a headache and a mild fever while they were in Florida, and toward the end of the trip he had suddenly stopped speaking entirely. They decided to bring him to the hospital as soon as they got home.

When I evaluated Bobby, his mental status was strikingly abnormal. He would not speak or answer any questions, suggesting diffuse brain damage, perhaps caused by encephalitis (swelling of the brain due to an infection). I was not surprised that Bobby had developed a serious infection, since his CD4 count had been dropping in recent weeks, leaving him susceptible to opportunistic pathogens. There were many possible causes for his symptoms. Some Florida lakes are known for a parasite that can infect the brain after an individual dives into the water and pushes the parasite into the sinuses through the nose. Herpes and toxoplasmosis are also common causes of serious infection in AIDS patients.

Bobby was admitted to the hospital, and I ordered a battery of tests to determine what might be causing his infection. We performed a lumbar puncture, putting a needle in between the vertebrae of the back to obtain fluid from the spinal canal to look for white blood cells, bacteria, fungi, or other signs of infection. We also obtained an MRI and an X-ray to look for abnormalities in the brain. However, upon review, all of Bobby's test results were completely normal. The fluid from his lumbar puncture was clean: no white blood cells and no other signs of infection (such as low glucose or high protein). His MRI showed the brain to be entirely normal. Surprised, I went to Bobby's room to get more details of the case history and to discuss the test results with his family.

When I arrived to deliver the news, the small hospital room was a disaster area of sorrow, anger, and fear. Bobby's parents were shouting at John, who had come to the hospital as Bobby's durable power of attorney for healthcare. He was the person we had called to get permission for the lumbar puncture, since Bobby was not able to make decisions for himself. The parents were telling John that, while on vacation, Bobby had been to a pastor. He had reavowed his religious convictions and renounced his homosexuality. He had also renounced John. John expressed his love for Bobby, seeming more hurt and humiliated than angry, but the parents were livid. Emotions were running high, and with no solution to their conflict in sight, they all turned to me: to cure the patient, to comfort the family, and to support the care-giver.

Through it all, Bobby had remained completely mute. But he seemed alert. I tried to engage him.

"Bobby, do you hear this?"

"Do you hear this," he answered. It was the first time he had spoken since admission.

"Bobby, are you okay?" I asked.

"Are you okay?" he answered.

"Are you awake?"

"Awake."

With a distant expression, Bobby could do nothing but repeat the words that were spoken to him. It is a condition called echolalia. While it can occur with brain disease, it is more often a symptom of a psychiatric disorder.

Stay calm, for this is much more complicated than anything infectious. I was not a psychiatrist, but I did not need to be. The dilemma was clear to me. The young man must have desperately wanted his parents' approval in Florida. He wanted the religion that he had been exposed to in his youth. He might indeed have experienced the conversion his parents had described. However, as the trip came to a close he knew he had to face a boyfriend that he also cared for. He could not disappoint his parents or the pastor, but neither could he give up John whom he clearly loved. Torn, he had become mute. He could not or would not speak.

I became very detached and tried to analyze the problem as if it were an infectious disease. I explained to everyone in the room that Bobby was not suffering from an infection, that his diagnosis was psychiatric. I assured John, Bobby, and his parents that we would get Bobby the psychiatric help that he needed. I tried to explain that this was no one's fault, but that it was a problem for all of us to solve together.

Bobby's parents did not appreciate my neutrality, but John was on board. He had come to expect that I would make no judgment about their lifestyle. Bobby was wild-eyed, pathetic, and ever so mute.

We transferred Bobby to a psychiatric hospital, and in two days he began speaking again. He tried to articulate his obvious dilemma and explain how helpless he felt, not wanting to cause pain to anyone he loved. John forgave him quickly. His parents needed more time. But Bobby's health, both mental and physical, was much improved, and he was released from the hospital shortly after.

In times of crisis, no matter the nature, a physician must do his best to promote calm, rational solutions to any problem. Even when emotions are running high and a situation is getting out of control, a physician must stay impassive and composed, and practice clear judgment. Despite the storm that brewed around me, despite the anger, sorrow, and fear that filled the room, I was able to act in my patient's best interest and promote reconciliation and peace.

In 1997, I was involved in a research project at the medical school in East Tennessee. We were testing the theory that vigorous exercise could improve the immunologic profile of a patient in a way that would help prevent cardiovascular disease. I was both an investigator and a volunteer subject for the study. Every few days I would ride a stationary bicycle twenty-five miles and then have my blood drawn to measure various chemicals in the bloodstream. Several weeks into the study, I passed the immunology laboratory, where the work was being done, on my way to giving a lecture for our medical students. I asked the lab tech how the study was going and he was enthusiastic about its progress.

"But, Dr. Berk, you need to get checked. Your hematocrit is over 60!"

"George, over 60, that's so abnormal. Please recheck it."

"Oh, I repeated it," he said. "Yes, over 60."

"Well, please check it again."

"Okay," he said with some hesitation.

I proceeded to my lecture at the hospital down the street.

The hematocrit level is used to measure the proportion of red blood cells in the blood. For adult men, it should be around 40, and 60 is highly unusual. A hematocrit of 60 meant that my body was massively overproducing red blood cells. There were only a few explanations for having a number so high, and I began to consider what the problem might be. Sometimes chronic smokers have high hematocrit levels because they develop breathing problems that cause perpetually low oxygen levels in their blood; increased production of red blood cells is a secondary effect. I was not a smoker and had never experienced breathing problems on my frequent runs or while biking for the study. Cancer can cause high hematocrit levels. A tumor in the kidney or the liver will cause the body to overproduce red blood cells in response. But I felt completely healthy and couldn't imagine that the diagnosis was cancer. No, clearly this had to be primary. I noted that I had been having lots of headaches recently, and that my blood pressure had been slightly higher than normal the last time I checked. These were probably the first signs of polycythemia vera, a chronic disorder of unknown origin that causes the bone marrow to overproduce red blood cells.

I arrived a minute early for my lecture and ducked into the

bathroom to feel for my spleen, which becomes enlarged in patients with polycythemia vera. It appeared normal, though it is difficult and unusual for physicians to perform such an exam on themselves. I knew it could not be cancer, but I went ahead and checked my liver (which is much easier to self-examine). It was normal. For the sake of thoroughness, I even attempted to feel for a kidney, but that organ is difficult to find in anyone. For all I could tell, I was in good health, but my hematocrit level was just too unusual to be normal. So I accepted the most likely diagnosis: polycythemia vera.

The symptoms of polycythemia usually appear in affected patients by the age of forty, and usually the course of the disease is not life threatening. However, some patients do develop acute myelogenous leukemia, a dangerous cancer generated in the bone marrow. Polycythemia patients are more likely to experience heart failure, or develop blood clots that can cause strokes and heart attacks.[2] However, with careful follow-up, polycythemia patients can live many years without initial treatment. I would be okay. I had seen many patients face lifelong illness with equanimity and nobility. I could certainly do the same.

On my way into lecture, I thought about telling Shirley about my prognosis later that night and planned to call the office of a close colleague, a hematologist, to set up an appointment. But for now I had a lecture to present to a hall crowded with students, so I pulled myself together. My lecture on meningitis went smoothly, as I listened to the cases presented by the residents and made suggestions on diagnosis and treatment. I also went over cases that I had seen and showed stained samples of spinal fluid to explain how one could quickly determine an etiologic agent. At the end of the lecture, I accepted the scattered applause and packed up to go. I was proud that I had completed my first lecture even as I had, within the past hour, diagnosed myself as having a chronic disease.

I headed back to the medical school, walking quickly to convince myself that I was in good physical condition. The lab tech that I had spoken with was waiting for me. He looked glum, much like I would have expected of someone who had to be the bearer of bad news.

"Dr. Berk, I am really, really sorry. I don't know how we got those results, but they are inaccurate. Your hematocrit is normal."

Of course I felt foolish, jumping to such far-fetched conclusions with so little information, examining myself in the men's room, and planning my life with a chronic disease. But at least I had not cancelled my lecture or called my wife in a panic. I had carried out the job of a physician, keeping sound judgment and composure throughout the two hours of my affliction. Osler would have been proud of my mastery of aequanimitas.

But learning aequanimitas is a lifelong task, and I have not always been completely successful. Over the years, some of my colleagues have pointed out that during difficult meetings or times of conflict among faculty, I will wring my hands, as if I am washing them at an imaginary sink. It is a sign that while externally I may have things under control, I am experiencing internal turmoil. At times in my career this symptom of stress has been particularly frequent. When I went down to East Tennessee from Boston, I rose in the ranks to become chief of medicine after only three years. As a leader among my colleagues, I had to advise and counsel physicians many years older than me. My new chief of cardiology, a famous researcher, was so arrogant and condescending that I could feel the blood rush to my face after every interaction I had with him. Out of curiosity, I once checked my blood pressure after one of his visits and was not surprised to find that my systolic was twenty points above normal.

But disagreeable colleagues were not the only source of anxiety. At East Tennessee, I had the honor of being chosen by the graduating students as the faculty member who would hood them at their graduation ceremony. I performed the duty for ten out of my eighteen years on staff. The graduation ceremony at ETSU is a massive event. Every year, students from the undergraduate, graduate, and medical school programs—over nine hundred in all—gathered with their friends and families in Johnson City's indoor football stadium. In front of a crowd of thousands, I stood on the giant stage and placed an honorary sash over the heads of our sixty graduating medical students. I was the first person to be able to say, "Congratulations, Dr. Allen," as each student came up and officially earned their MD. Some students seized the moment with great pride, tears in their eyes and a hand raised in victory. Others just wanted to get back to their seats.

I would have been in the latter category. Even with ten years of experience, I still worried about tripping over my gown, knocking off the hat of a graduate, or just looking foolish in front of the crowd. Sometimes I could feel my legs shaking as I performed the ceremony. Aequanimitas was my goal, but I was probably more successful at maintaining composure in the hospital and clinic than in my personal life.

Having convinced the gunman to stay in the car, I enter my house alone. My wife is standing in the middle of the very large kitchen, focused on various salad ingredients lined up along the countertop. It is a routine, very sunny, spring morning. For her sake, I must appear calm. I must be imperturbable. I must have Osler's aequanimitas.

When I enter, I am dressed in shorts and a T-shirt, but since I jog on Sunday mornings she does not suspect anything unusual. I give her a quick, confident, friendly hello, and pass through the kitchen heading for the bedroom. I pray that Shirley will not ask questions and that the man in my garage will not decide to follow me into the house. My only goal is to get in and out with as much cash and valuables as I can find so that this stranger will leave me and my family alone forever. I go straight for my wife's jewelry box and take out the first drawer, which is filled with expensive-looking gemstone rings.

At the time, I don't think about what I am taking from my wife. I don't see her high school ring, or her mom's heirlooms. I don't notice the ring we chose at an international symposium in Hawaii after hours of shopping that left my feet aching, or the blue and gold ring I designed myself to represent the ETSU colors. In that moment, material objects have no importance to me; all I can think is that the rings together look very valuable, like a treasure chest of gems. The gunman will be satisfied. He will take them from me along with whatever cash I find, and then he will let me go.

On my way back through the kitchen, I force myself to smile cheerfully, telling myself to stay calm and natural the entire time. I don't pause, since I have no time to lie about why I have been in her jewelry drawer. Before exiting out the back door, I take her wallet out of her purse on the counter. Earlier in the day, it held twenty-two dollars, but she gave up the twenty at church. There are two singles left for the robber's fund.

To my great relief and surprise, Shirley says nothing and continues cooking. She notices my strange behavior, but thinks, I learn later, that I am buying her a ring. I need her jewelry drawer to see what she already has, and I need the credit card from her purse to make a big purchase.

State of Texas v. Jack Lindsey Jordan

> DISTRICT ATTORNEY BLOUNT: At some point that morning did something out of the ordinary happen?
>
> SHIRLEY BERK: Well, I was there in the kitchen and Steve came running through the kitchen and said don't ask any questions, smiling, and so I didn't think anything about it. And then he went to the bedroom, because he ran back out with the top drawer of my jewelry box, which had rings in it, and then he ran back out. And he got my wallet from my purse, which was there on the kitchen counter.
>
> BLOUNT: Okay, and when he came in and got your jewelry drawer and wallet you didn't think anything was out of the ordinary?
>
> SHIRLEY: Well, he said don't ask questions, and I guess I don't know what I was thinking. I thought maybe he was taking my jewelry box to see what rings I had and didn't have.
>
> BLOUNT: So he could get you something new?
>
> SHIRLEY: Right.

I'm relieved that Shirley doesn't suspect anything. I'm grateful that I was able to stay calm under the incredible emotional strain of bringing this man back to my home, of putting my wife in such imminent danger. But years of being a physician have taught me to control my emotions, to push back fear and uncertainty and do what needs to be done.

State of Texas v. Jack Lindsey Jordan

DISTRICT ATTORNEY EVANS, Closing Argument:

I was recently hospitalized for a pretty serious illness and I made it through. I made it through due to people with even temperament and calm, cool, collected demeanor—the nurses and the doctors of the hospital where I was. I made it through because of the way they are. They were able to keep their heads together. They were able to save me from further harm. And that's what Dr. Berk did on that day.

You know, I'm not as calm, cool, and collected as Dr. Berk is, and most people aren't. But you know what? That saved not only himself that day, but it saved his wife that day from any harm. It saved his son that day from any harm and God forbid death, and it saved any innocent bystander from this man who's driving around with his shotgun pointed not only to his face but his back.

Glad that Shirley is safe, I collect my robber's loot and return to the garage. I have been gone for only seconds. As I promised, I was in the house and back out in a minute. When I get back to the car, the kidnapper has switched to the driver's seat, so I get in on the passenger's side.

Some people may question how I was ever able to get back into that car with my abductor. He let me go, and I should have made a run for it. But no, *We have a deal,* I think. *I have kept my end of the bargain. Now, he will keep his. He will let me out down the street and this ordeal will be over.*

State of Texas v. Jack Lindsey Jordan

> DISTRICT ATTORNEY BLOUNT: Explain why you did what
> he wanted you to do.
>
> STEVEN BERK: Right. I mean obviously I thought to close the
> garage door, lock the door, call 911, but I didn't think that
> was the best bet. I felt like I could get out of this okay, and I
> didn't want to put my wife in jeopardy. And I had no doubt
> that if it had been much longer he would come through the
> house with his gun. It seemed like it was best to go back to
> the car. He had moments of anger, but we had also talked,
> and I still thought I had a pretty good chance just doing
> what he said to do, that it would turn out okay.

Up to this point in my kidnapping, I have survived by trusting my instincts. I have controlled my fear and acted calmly, trying to base every action on reason and clear judgment. Because I have kept my calm, this intruder has come to trust me. At this point, it doesn't make sense to violate the trust of such a hostile person. I get back in the car because that is our deal. Though I still consider him dangerous, this man is no longer a stranger.

6

The Patient

I get back in the SUV on the passenger's side. As the gunman drives out of our subdivision and back toward the main streets of Amarillo, I expect him to stop and let me out of the car at any moment. Freedom and safety, I think, are literally around the corner. I notice that the streets are now much more crowded with cars and people and realize suddenly that it is noon. Amarillo is coming to life as people stream out of church and head for Sunday brunch.

The gunman shows no sign of stopping, and I begin to worry. We have a deal, an arrangement that the defense attorney at the trial will later call a "gentleman's agreement." But this man is far from gentle, and I begin to feel foolish for relying on his word. We keep driving.

"You said you would let me go."

"But not here, not with people around. And I still haven't filled up with gas."

Yes, filling up with gas has always been part of the plan. I wait anxiously for what will come next. There's nothing else for me to do.

He gets back on Bell Street and then makes a left turn, heading west on Thirty-fourth Street. He doesn't really know where he's going. We pass several gas stations, but they're too exposed and crowded. Thirty-fourth Street is a wide, busy thoroughfare, not a place where he wants to stop for gas and probably not where he would even consider letting me go.

"Not here," he says as we pass another gas station on the right.

We keep heading west, and the traffic lights begin to be spaced farther and farther apart. We are reaching the outskirts of Amarillo.

I begin to panic, terrified that he is not going to let me go as he promised. "Let me out right here," I plead. I want desperately to get out of the car, to disappear into a corner fire station, call home and end this ordeal. Suddenly I feel cold, despite the afternoon sunshine. There is no air-conditioning in the car, but the window is cracked and I start to shiver. We are leaving Amarillo, driving farther west down Thirty-fourth Street than I have ever been before. Beyond the outskirts of town there is nothing but open fields. *The ideal place to kill someone,* I imagine.

When Jordan came through my garage, one of the books gathering dust on the bookcase he passed was Joseph Wambaugh's *The Onion Field.* I had read it years before, a terrifying story of a kidnapping. The two criminals who took the officer thought that kidnapping was a capital crime in California, that they already faced the death penalty just for forcing the officer into their car. Convinced that there was no reason to let him live, they shot their captive several times and abandoned his body in that deserted onion field.

We reach the intersection of Thirty-fourth and Soncy Road, the last traffic light to the west of Amarillo. The light turns green, and the gunman speeds out into the open countryside. We pass fields of long grass and grazing cattle. The SUV bounces violently over the uneven road, which is lined with long ditches, occasional barbed-wire fences, and a long string of telephone poles, tall crosses that stretch ominously into the distance. The land is completely flat, and the sky is endlessly blue. As we pass, yellow-bellied finches fly up out of the tall grass, and I envy their freedom. I can see a farmhouse on the horizon, barely visible from the road. But as far as I can tell, there isn't another human being for miles around.

I contemplate what I'll do if he takes me out into one of these fields. *I could make a run for it.* I'm in good physical condition from running several miles every day, and I consider the option of sprinting across the open fields in search of help. Not for the first time that day, the terrifying prospect of being shot in the back sends a chill down my spine. *I could fight for possession of the gun.* On my side would be the element of surprise. He doesn't think I'm a physical threat, and I've been nothing but compliant all morning. He wouldn't expect me to make a move for his shotgun.

I take a look at him. We're the same size—almost. But I'm skeptical. Except for the emergency room tussle at BCH, I haven't been in a fight since 1965.

It was in the hallway of my high school back in New Jersey. We were on our way to AP English class, and for some reason Joey Mimich decided to push me into the girls' bathroom. It was a harmless prank, but I really didn't want to go in there. A shoving match ensued, and suddenly we were grappling with each other, knocking into other students and causing a traffic jam in the hallway. Surprisingly, I threw the first actual punch to Joey's midsection. The fight was stopped moments later by Mrs. Soulter, who broke us up, hustled us into her classroom, and told us sternly to take our seats. The bell rang, and she began her lecture. For the next forty-five minutes, Joey and I had to sweat it out, wondering what our punishment would be. Fighting was immediate grounds for suspension at my school, and I cringed to think of the phone call home to my parents and the headline that would certainly appear in the school newspaper the following week: "Top Student Bruised, Suspended in Hallway Brawl." *When asked why he jeopardized his academic career by throwing a punch, Berk answered, "I did not want to be pushed into the ladies' room."*

After class, Mrs. Soulter chastised us for being hooligans, but she did not report the fight to our principal. I was grateful and took her lecture that "violence is not the answer" to heart. Forty years later, as I contemplate attacking this criminal and taking his gun, I'm still convinced that physical violence is not my best option. I commit myself once again to staying calm in the face of danger, knowing that it's my surest chance of getting out of this situation alive and unharmed.

As we get farther from the busy streets of Amarillo, the gunman seems to relax. He shifts in the driver's seat, leaning back a little bit and letting his foot fall heavily on the accelerator. As we hit open road, he suddenly begins a conversation.

"My back is killing me, Berk," he says. He complains of chronic pain and tells me about his recent back surgery. "It was back in July, but it didn't help. My back still hurts, and now I can't get by without the pain meds they gave me after the operation."

Listen to his complaint and make suggestions, I think to myself.

"Back pain is an awful problem," I tell him. "I know what it's like, and I'm sorry for you. Being under stress only makes things worse." *Yes, being a kidnapper must be very stressful.*

I ask him how he has tried to manage the pain (self-medication) and what types of exercises he has done as rehab after his surgery (none). I listen to his symptoms and make suggestions about treatment options. It's not a ploy to curry favor or gain his trust. It's not even an attempt to gather information about him (though it crosses my mind that the date of his surgery might be used to identify him later). No, I enter the conversation instinctively, without thinking of its implications. I'm a physician, and that's what I have been trained to do. I try to ignore the miles of empty space that stretch out around us in every direction and listen to what he has to say.

The gunman seems to appreciate the conversation. He appears less paranoid and begins to speak more freely.

"Berk," he says. "I used to love Berk and Ernie. Did you ever watch Berk and Ernie as a kid?"

"That was Bert and Ernie," I reply.

"No, it was Berk and Ernie," he says.

I choose not to argue, and we drive the next mile in silence.

A minute later, he speaks up again.

"I'm a really good person," he tells me unexpectedly. A few seconds later he adds, "When I'm not on drugs."

I don't reply, but wait attentively for what will come next.

"You know I lost my wife," he continues. "And I was blamed for her death."

He tells the short but tragic story. They were in Memphis, Tennessee, and he was driving in his car with his wife in the passenger seat. He lost control of the car, and she was thrown out through the windshield as the vehicle spun around several times at high speed.

As he describes the accident I glance at the speedometer. We're going over sixty miles per hour down a bumpy dirt road, and he's not paying much attention to his driving. *Listen, make suggestions.* He continues.

"After the accident, they said it was intentional, that I was trying to kill her. They called it murder." He becomes tearful and expresses profound remorse over losing his wife.

"Imagine wanting to kill her. I loved my wife. She loved me."

"Sounds like you really cared about her," I say. "It would be awful to be blamed for harming your wife if it was just an accident. That would be too much to bear."

He agrees, and tells me that he was accused and convicted of manslaughter, that he was sent to prison because they called his accident a crime.

"Prison was an awful place. It only made me go downhill with more drugs and more rage. I tried to get help there, but no one can help you. You just try to survive."

"Why are you committing a crime now?" I ask him.

"A parole violation, not filling out the right forms, just a small mistake. But it forced me to run."

He tells me that his current flight from the law is the result of a technicality, an unsigned paper, an unpaid fee. I sympathize with him. I have known patients, students, and colleagues whose lives have spiraled out of control because of misfortune and mistakes.

"You need help," I tell him. I'm thinking about other patients I've treated. In my career, I've taken care of sociopaths, forgers, drug addicts, prisoners, drunk drivers, and more. I treated them all, trying to end their pain or save their lives. As a physician, it has never been my place to judge or discriminate, but simply to help and to heal when I can.

"Who will help me, Berk?"

"A doctor, a counselor. There are always people willing to help."

"Like you?" he asks.

I pause. I have helped others like him, but I'm suddenly repulsed at the thought of saying anything that might give the impression that I would ever voluntarily prolong our relationship. If he had come to see me in clinic, I would have done everything in my power to help him. I would have treated his drug addiction as a disease and gotten him the emotional guidance that he needed. But this man did not come to me in the hospital. He invaded my home and threatened my family. I cannot tell him, "Yes, like me."

State of Texas v. Jack Lindsey Jordan

DEFENSE ATTORNEY BAILEY: Didn't Mr. Jordan tell you about his history?

BERK: Yes.

BAILEY: And didn't you have a long conversation about that?

BERK: I don't think it was that long, but yes, he told me about his wife.

BAILEY: And did you not feel like you had a client patient relationship with him there for a while?

BERK: Yes sir.

BAILEY: Have you ever heard of robbing somebody and kidnapping them and then telling them their whole life story?

DISTRICT ATTORNEY BLOUNT: Objection as to relevance.

JUDGE: Sustained.

. . .

> DISTRICT ATTORNEY BLOUNT: Okay. You were asked some questions and testified that there was some normal conversation in the car. There was talk of his wife and things of that nature.
>
> BERK: Yes.
>
> BLOUNT: And you engaged in this quote, unquote normal kind of conversation. Is that right? Why were you interested in engaging in some normal conversation?
>
> BERK: I mean, I don't know if I was thinking about it in that way. Obviously the more normal the conversation, the better it was for me. But there was . . . There was, you know, the patient-physician thing that we are just trained to do. That was . . . well, real.

"Like you?" he asks again. I still cannot answer. "You would help me under other circumstances," he says, answering his own question correctly. He briefly makes eye contact and almost grins. "I bet you would have just loaned me the money."

"I've loaned people money before," I reply. My wife knows I've spent a fortune on loans, many never repaid, to students and residents who came asking for help. Yes, over the years I've even given money to a patient or two.

He asks me what religion I am.

It's a complicated question for me, but I give him the safest answer: Methodist, the religion of my wife and children.

"When I let you go, you can never tell anyone about me."

"That's fine," I enthusiastically agree. I promise to say nothing about what has happened.

"I would come back, kill you and kill your family," he says matter-of-factly.

The unexpected statement makes my heart race. Over the past

few minutes, we have established a fragile relationship. I think he sees value in himself through me, and perhaps has some respect for doctors. I pity him for his misfortune, but he is still terrifying.

"Why do you have to say things like that?" I ask with disappointment. I want to say, *You sure know how to kill a conversation.*

"I'll know if you talk," he says, ignoring my response. "I can check on what I'm charged with."

My heart beats even faster. This man has committed so many crimes that he checks for updates on his latest known offense, like a professor might check Medline, a computerized collection of journal articles that can be used to confirm a researcher's latest publications. I wonder what else this man has done.

As he's driving, I notice two deep cuts over the knuckles of his right hand.

I'm reminded of a patient I saw while I was still in residency at Boston City Hospital. He came into the emergency room complaining of fever and chills. When I examined him, I noticed that his hand was swollen and red, and there were cuts on his knuckles. I asked him what had happened, and he replied that a drunk person bit him the night before in a bar. I accepted his explanation without thinking much more of it and prescribed an antibiotic for his fever that would fight all the bacteria normally found in the human mouth. I presented the case on rounds, describing the wound and the patient's explanation to my fellow residents and my attending. They were amused. Bitten? Everyone on the team but me realized that the patient had punched someone in the mouth.

I glance again at the injured hand clutching the steering wheel. *So my captor has been in a recent fistfight.* I don't want to think of him as a violent man. I prefer to imagine that he is a desperate and reluctant criminal, driven to crime by misfortune rather than by his violent and aggressive nature. His tearful history suggests that crime was the unplanned result of misfortune, but his behavior is consistent with that of a sociopath, an antisocial and remorseless person who has no regard for society's laws and customs.

We are well outside of Amarillo now, still speeding past deserted fields. We haven't passed a gas station, and I wonder if he knows where he's going or if he has a plan for what he'll do next. The bruises on his knuckles bother me, and I can't decide whether this man is a patient or a criminal.

State of Texas v. Jack Lindsey Jordan

DISTRICT ATTORNEY EVANS: Back in 2005 you were acquainted with a gentleman that you knew by the name of Jack.

WHIT: Yes ma'am.

EVANS: And did there come an event sometime a week or two before March 5 that you and Jack had some words.

WHIT: Uh huh.

EVANS: And what happened?

WHIT: Well, he had come over, and we were visiting and I had a girlfriend coming over and I wanted to be by myself with her, and I told him to go. And he didn't want to go, so we got into an argument.

EVANS: After you had words that day, when was the next time you saw him?

WHIT: Around 1:30–2:00 p.m., Saturday afternoon [March 5]. I heard a car door, and I looked out my window, and I could see the SUV that he was using at the time. I figured there was going to be an argument, so I met him at the door. I told him I had my girlfriend here and he needed to go. He just looked at me and said "All right." I turned around and was headed back to my bedroom. And the next thing I knew I heard my screen door open. I came around the corner. He was standing a few feet inside the house unwrapping a gun. There was definitely something wrong with the way he was looking at me. And I just went and grabbed the barrel of the gun. I had the barrel and he was still holding onto it. He was hitting me with his right hand on the left side of my face and back of my head. He couldn't let go of the gun to get my legs off of him, and I couldn't let go of the gun to do anything else. I was getting real dizzy, and the blood from hitting me in the face was starting to sting, and I was getting light-headed. I could feel myself fading fast.

EVANS: Did you eventually pass out?

WHIT: Yes ma'am.

EVANS: Did you have to go to the hospital as a result of the injuries you received?

WHIT: Yes Ma'am.

EVANS: And what type of injuries did you have as a result?

WHIT: My face was laid open in several places. The bone of my eye socket on the side of my head was chipped.

EVANS: How long did you have to stay in the hospital?

WHIT: The better part of three days.

EVANS: And what kind of treatment did you receive?

WHIT: I had an MRI. I had stitches all over my face and head.

EVANS: Do you still have scars to this day from the injuries that you received?

WHIT: Yes ma'am.

According to the American Psychiatric Association's *Diagnostic and Statistical Manual of Mental Disorders*, patients with antisocial personality disorder—sociopaths—show characteristic behavioral patterns:

1. Failure to conform to social norms with respect to lawful behavior, as indicated by repeatedly performing acts that are grounds for arrest.

    Whether or not his parole violation was a technicality, this man is a repeat offender.

2. Impulsivity or failure to plan ahead.

    I think about our erratic drive through Amarillo and his impulsive directions.

3. Reckless disregard for the safety of self or others.

    We are still speeding down a bumpy dirt road. Earlier, when I asked him what the chances were that the shotgun could go off in my back by accident, he was amused.

4. Irritability and aggressiveness as indicated by repeated physical fights.

    Yes, that cut is over the knuckle.

5. Lack of remorse, as indicated by being indifferent to or rationalizing having hurt, mistreated, or stolen from another.

    He does not see me as his victim.

As a physician I try not to judge, only to help. I've known many patients who are sociopaths, but I've never been at the mercy of one until today.

We pass a sign for Bushland, a small town about twenty miles west of Amarillo. By confirming with my diagnostic skills that my abductor is a sociopath, I have frightened myself.

Dr. Steven Berk
Born: New York City, New York, Population 9,000,000
Died: Bushland, Texas, Population 430

7

Mistakes

Y ou know, I'm the last person that would hurt anyone," he
says as we enter Bushland.

I stay silent. I suspect that he's hurt people before.

"I was pushed into this by some mistakes," he tells me. "My
wife's death was my big mistake, and then the drugs, the worst
mistake. But there are small mistakes, like parole violation," he
says, with special bitterness.

"Well, we all can make mistakes," I say, almost patronizingly,
wondering if I've kept the bitterness out of my own voice. Mistakes? He uses the word as if it absolves him of responsibility for
what he has done. Perhaps he considers this very kidnapping a
mistake, but there's no sign that he has any intention of correcting it. He wants to believe he is a good person, forced by circumstances to do bad things. For a moment, I resent my participation
in his self-serving rationalization.

"You, Berk. Have you made mistakes?"

I pause. *Yes,* I think to myself, *I've made mistakes. I left my ga-*

rage door open this morning, but if I survive this, I will not do it again.

I don't answer him, but I consider the many mistakes I've made in my own life. Medicine is a profession with very little room for error, and the mistakes of a physician can be dire indeed. Some of my mistakes have come at a very high cost, but they are the dues I've paid for competence. As a physician, I have always tried to do the right thing, to give my patients the best possible care. But I have faltered, and sometimes I have failed. Yes, of course I have made mistakes, large and small, and I take responsibility for them. But whether the mistakes are now just embarrassing memories or deeply felt, lifelong regrets, I try to see each one as a lesson, as an opportunity to be both a better physician and a better person.

I started medical school at Boston University in 1971 with the intention of doing research in the field of muscular dystrophy. I had just spent my last summer with Pat and Kevin, and I had a passionate desire to do something. At the time, physicians were largely powerless to provide any type of treatment for patients with muscular dystrophy. Only further research on the disease could provide hope that, one day, treatments would be available to improve and extend the lives of children like Pat and Kevin. From my many years at Camp Merry Heart, I had intimate knowledge of the human experience of the disease, but I also spent the summer before medical school learning about the science behind it. I read journal articles about all that was known about the causes of and potential cures for muscular dystrophy, and I got in touch with Dr. William Ullrich, a basic researcher in Boston who agreed to mentor me in my work as a first-year medical student.

I had designed an experiment to test the theory that growth

hormones might have an effect on the rate of muscle deterioration in dystrophic mice. Dr. Ullrich approved of my plans but informed me that the only place to get dystrophic mice was from the Bar Harbor Laboratories in Maine. You had to request them from the laboratory director there and make a strong case for the legitimacy of your research aims as well as your interest and enthusiasm in this field. As a first-year medical student, my chances were not good, but Dr. Ullrich encouraged me to make a phone call and send a follow-up letter describing the experiments in detail. I had not moved into my apartment in Boston yet, and so I made the phone call from the hotel where I was staying.

Someone answered the phone almost immediately, and I went right into the speech I had prepared.

"Hello, my name is Steven Berk, and I'm calling because I need your help. I want to be a part of the research that will eventually help find a cure for muscular dystrophy. I've worked with children with muscular dystrophy for eight years, and I've seen them enjoy life, struggle with their disease, and eventually die. I understand the disease because I've lived with it day and night. I want to give the children who are still living with muscular dystrophy hope for the future, and I believe the only way to do that is through research. My experiments can only be done with your dystrophic mice, and there is no other way to test my theories of the disease." At this point, the woman on the other end of the line started to interrupt me, but I wouldn't let her. I had to make sure all of my passion for the project was laid out clearly. "I request your help. I am passionate about my work. I don't want to fail these children, who show so much courage just by living their lives every day. I don't want to fail the memory of others who have already died from this terrible disease. Please help me do this important research so that we can find a cure together."

There was silence on the line, and then a sniff. I could tell that I was convincing, and I waited for her response expectantly. Her voice broke as she tearfully replied, "I'm only the hotel operator, but I will do anything I can to help you."

Of course, my mistake did not have any bad consequences. It was a simple error, the result of my enthusiasm and a lack of equanimity. Fortunately, I did end up getting the mice from Bar Harbor, perhaps because I had the chance to practice my impassioned speech on someone else first. I completed my experiments and published my first paper as a second-year medical student. Unfortunately, my idea did not work. However, as with all mistakes and failures, my experiments were not for nothing. In science and in life, sometimes our failures teach us just as much as our successes.

Mr. Mercante was assigned as my patient when I was a resident at Boston City Hospital. He had been admitted for persistent chest pain, but tests had shown that he had not had a heart attack. When I examined him, I realized that there was a major problem with his heart valve. Heart valve abnormalities cause distinctive heart sounds, and through my stethoscope I could hear the distinctive rough sound over his heart and radiating to his neck. By palpating his chest, I could feel that his heart was enlarged. Physical examination also revealed that his carotid arteries were very weak, another characteristic symptom. The diagnosis was definite: aortic stenosis, an abnormality of one of the heart valves. Ultrasound imaging confirmed my suspicion, revealing a very severe narrowing of Mr. Mercante's aorta near the valve that leads to the heart. The narrowing was restricting blood flow to the heart and causing his chest pain. Without immediate correction, blood supply would be so restricted that the heart muscle would begin to die of oxygen deprivation, and Mr. Mercante would almost certainly die of a heart attack.

I discussed Mr. Mercante's case with my attending.

"We could correct the stenosis with open-heart valve replacement surgery, but he's eighty-two years old. I don't know if such a risky procedure would be worth it at his age. Still, without treatment, the stenosis will certainly kill him."

My attending told me to review the literature, to find out whether older patients responded well to corrective surgery. I was somewhat surprised by the results. Opinions on the subject were unanimous: experts recommended surgery across the board. There could be complications—especially in older patients—but in most cases even eighty-year-olds had a better chance of survival if they underwent the procedure.

I was ready to discuss options with Mr. Mercante at the bedside. I was still an intern in the early months of my medical training, but he was my patient, assigned to me just like the other nineteen patients I was caring for at the time. I had done thorough research. I gave him a detailed account of his options and then confidently delivered my opinion about what he should do.

"And so it would be my strong recommendation to pursue surgery for correcting the heart valve. It's risky, but not as risky as leaving the condition untreated. I believe surgery is the right course for you."

"I'm too old for surgery. I have no interest in the idea," replied Mr. Mercante.

"I understand, but I think we should keep an open mind about this. You are so healthy otherwise, and we have experienced cardiac surgeons who would give you the best possible care."

"Thank you for your opinion, but I'm not interested."

"If you were my dad, I would recommend this surgery." I was

convinced from the papers I had read, and I could not help push-ing what I believed was his best option. I was disappointed when he ended the discussion, still firm in his decision not to undergo the open-heart surgery. However, a couple of days later, he asked to speak with me.

"I want to know more," he said. "I want to talk to a surgeon, keep my options open."

I was pleased and immediately made the referral.

Later that day, my senior resident grabbed me in the hall.

"Steve, you need to talk to the chief resident. I think we have a problem."

Getting called in by the chief resident is like being called into the principal's office. The position of chief resident is high in the hospital hierarchy, just a step below faculty, and though I had a good relationship with my chief, I was nervous when I entered his office.

"You really messed up," the chief told me seriously.

"Okay, who did I kill?" I asked, nervously trying to make a joke.

"Worse than that," he replied, shaking his head. "Have you met the director of the outreach clinic, Dr. McGowan? He's an important faculty member."

"No, I don't know him."

"Yeah, well, he knows you now. He's Mercante's doctor. He's been following Mercante's aortic stenosis for years."

"But Mercante is my patient. He can't be McGowan's; he's on our ward. He was assigned to me."

"No, he's McGowan's. Mercante is an outreach patient who got put on our ward because of crowding. You should have checked the old records better."

"No, there were no notes from that clinic."

But I had made a mistake. Somehow I was supposed to know that this patient had a real doctor following him, a senior faculty member who was in charge of his care.

"Anyway, you convinced the patient to undergo surgery. You confused him. Surgery really hasn't been recommended for him."

"But it's the right choice. You know that. The surgery *is* recommended, even for the very elderly." My voice rose as I tried to defend my actions, but my chief resident was unmoved.

"Berk," he said with resignation, "call McGowan. Apologize. The guy is really angry. He wants you out of the program."

I made the call. McGowan was livid, and heatedly told me that I was out of line, that I had undermined the physician-patient relationship. I had humiliated him by going against his recommendations and his authority as Mercante's primary care physician.

I misguidedly tried to defend myself. "I think I gave him the right advice. All the literature supports doing the surgery."

"*Not* for Mercante," hissed McGowan.

The conversation was over. I had made things worse.

My senior resident came to see me after the phone call. "Steve, you need to be more diplomatic. You're an intern, and McGowan's faculty. It's no good making enemies of senior faculty like that. The chief said that if you weren't Boston U, you'd probably be gone."

I was not kicked out of my residency program, but I was taken off of Mr. Mercante's case. He was easily talked out of surgery, and he died just months later.

Perhaps I was right about standards of clinical practice, but I had still made a mistake. In the medical profession, there are protocols of conduct, respect for differences of opinion, and recognition of seniority that I had failed to abide by. Of course, patient care should always be my primary goal, but I had to learn that I couldn't help anybody if I got fired from my job for disrespecting my superiors. Part of being a physician was working within the hospital hierarchy and developing good relationships with my colleagues so that we could work together for our patients. Later in my career, I would remember that awful confrontation with McGowan and choose diplomacy to resolve conflict with my peers. I knew that no matter our differences of opinion, the health of the patient was always more important than our egos.

When I was a resident, everyone in the program at Boston City Hospital was required to spend two months out of their year working across the street at University Hospital. Some residents considered it a welcome break. Unlike BCH, University was a private hospital and so it served a much wealthier clientele. University was always kept bright and clean, and the cafeteria food was excellent. Paradoxically, the patients could be much more difficult to deal with. Many of them mistrusted interns and residents and preferred to be seen by the hospital's private doctors. Moreover, when a tragedy occurred, it sometimes hit closer to home, since residents could often better relate to the more privileged patients at University Hospital.

In my second year of residency, I was responsible for treating Mr. Goens at University. He was a fireman who had been admitted to the hospital with pneumonia and failing lungs, but I don't remember if his symptoms were related to his job as a fireman. Mr. and Mrs. Goens were great people, and I was glad to be helping with their case. I could never communicate very well directly with the patient, since he was on a ventilator throughout his hospital stay. But I had a very good relationship with his wife and tried to communicate all the details of her husband's condition and treatment so that she could share the information with him.

Mr. Goens was my sickest patient, and so I always paid special attention to him on rounds. He suffered from respiratory failure, kidney failure, pneumonia, diabetes, and other complications. Every day, I would carefully write my note, updating the status of each problem and including all of the new physical findings, patient symptoms, lab results, and X-rays. I took pride in the completeness of those notes: I knew that no matter how complicated things got, any physician covering Mr. Goens's case would know and understand exactly what was happening.

Each morning I would go over the note carefully with Mrs. Goens and explain each detail of her husband's progress. Every update was news to be celebrated.

"His creatinine levels are normal. We can stop dialysis."

"We're bringing down the oxygen levels on his ventilator every day. He'll be breathing on his own in a few weeks."

"Blood sugars are normal now. This is a good sign."

I was ecstatic about the success of my care. This critically ill patient was getting better, and there was new evidence of his healing every day. I had never seen a patient so ill respond so well, and I was proud to discuss every aspect of the patient's improvement with Mrs. Goens. She had told me that her husband loved fishing, so I would cheerfully tell Mr. Goens about how healthy he was becoming and how close to that next big fishing trip he was getting. For several weeks, visiting my sickest patient was the highlight of my day.

On an evening when I was off call, however, Mr. Goens's blood pressure dropped, and his breathing became labored and irregular. On rounds the next morning, my patient was unresponsive and his wife was panicked. I found a whole new list of problems on his chart and data that suggested that all his organs were failing at once. It was sepsis, a new infection that Mr. Goens had acquired from the hospital itself.

As before, I fought with his numbers, but this time nothing would improve. The patient required more oxygen, new medications to keep his blood pressure up, and special intravenous lines and monitoring equipment. He was often unconscious, but Mrs. Goens was a constant figure at his bedside. He was declining rapidly, and nothing I did seemed to make any difference. On morning rounds, I began to rush my evaluation of Mr. Goens, and I stopped taking time to discuss the details of his ever-deteriorating condition with his wife. I felt like I didn't have anything to offer either of them. What could I say? "You know all those things that were improving? Well, they're all worse than ever." Mr. Goens died about three weeks after developing sepsis, and during the entire period of his decline, I hardly spoke with Mrs. Goens. She knew her husband was dying without my telling her.

My attending on the case was a famous cardiologist and a good person. After the patient's death, he took me aside and critiqued my care.

"Berk, what were you thinking? You abandoned the wife when she needed you most. You went from being the most caring physician around to being almost invisible. I had to provide the support when you signed off the emotional aspect of the case."

"There was nothing I could do, nothing I could say to make him better." But I realized how foolish I sounded. I realized that even if there was nothing I could do to improve my patient's physical condition, I could have provided emotional support to him and his wife. I could have made his suffering and the prospect of his death easier to bear.

My attending was also unconvinced by my denial. "No, you could have done more. But you were ashamed. You were ashamed to admit that the patient was going to die under your care. You didn't want to face his wife and tell her you had failed. The truth is, Berk, you did the best you could in terms of treating the illness. But treating the patient, that's where you failed. You just weren't there for them when things took a turn for the worse, and that's when they needed you most."

It was too late to make amends. The patient was gone, the wife no longer around. I should have called, apologized, explained that I was new to this business. But I did not. A new sense of shame prevented me from seeking out Mrs. Goens and telling her how sorry I was. But I promised myself that I would learn from my mistake. A decade later, when the AIDS era turned my practice of medicine inside out, providing the proper emotional support was often the only treatment that I could offer my patients. I failed Mr. and Mrs. Goens, but never again did I check out emotionally on a patient.

Freddy was a patient who came to see me when I was practicing in Tennessee in 1985. He had been referred to me from the public health department after testing positive for HIV during a health screening. Freddy was in a high-risk group for contracting HIV and developing AIDS. His roommate had died of AIDS several months before, and Freddy had continued having unprotected sex with multiple gay partners even after his positive diagnosis. He also abused and sold cocaine and other drugs. However, despite his HIV diagnosis and drug problem, alcoholism was by far Freddy's biggest health concern.

Freddy was a frequent visitor to the emergency room for alcohol-related complications. Every time he arrived, I would make sure that his symptoms were not the result of an opportunistic infection contracted due to HIV. He arrived with symptoms of vomiting and diarrhea, and I ordered tests to rule out gastrointestinal infection. He would be delivered to the ER unconscious, and I performed exams that ruled out infection in the central nervous system. Invariably, his symptoms were the result of inebriation, and I did my best to convince him to get treatment for his drinking problem.

Over time, it became clear to me that Freddy was on a path of self-destruction. He would show up at my clinic without an appointment and often miss the clinic appointments that were scheduled. During his appointments, he showed a disturbing lack of concern, both for himself and others.

"So Freddy, how are you today?"

"I love your hair, Doc."

"Yes, well, I'm asking about your condition, your problems."

"So when can we go out?"

"I'm your doctor, Freddy, and I'm not gay. From the looks of your arms, you're still using drugs."

"Yes, and I know what you're going to say, but of course we share needles. Doesn't everyone?"

"You'll give someone AIDS, Freddy."

"Not my problem."

"And unprotected sex?"

"Still. All the time. They love me. I'm always the receiver. I love when you ask me that."

"You're putting yourself at risk for contracting other diseases. And you could give HIV to someone else. You know I'll have to report you again." At that time, we were required to inform the state health department if an HIV-positive patient reported a history of unprotected sex.

Freddy did not seem to care. "Have you thought about fixing up your office a bit, Doc? You know, make it more colorful?"

"Freddy, I don't want to have to come see you here or in the ER because you're drunk."

"But Doc, that's your job, that's what you get paid to do."

"I can have you discharged as a patient. I just have to give you notice."

"No, Doc, you know that's not right. You have to find me another doctor and there's no one else taking AIDS patients outside your group." He was right. Freddy was the most difficult patient at our practice, and we never once got reimbursed for his care. (He worked part-time, so he was ineligible for Medicaid, and he simply never paid his many medical bills.) But no matter how difficult or futile caring for him seemed, the truth was that no one else in the area would treat HIV-positive patients. There was truly nowhere else for him to go.

"Freddy, your CD4 count is still good, but you can't keep abusing your body this way. The drugs and especially the alcohol are going to compromise your health, and long term, combined with the HIV, they'll kill you."

"Still love you; you look great when you're mad."

After that visit, Freddy disappeared from clinic for a while. During the weeks he was gone, a new test had become available to us for diagnosing HIV. The test that had originally given Freddy his positive diagnosis was known for giving false positives (it was used because of its very low rate of false negatives), and a new method had been developed for diagnosing the disease. The new test had inspired a lot of public discussion about the effects of an inaccurate diagnosis of HIV. In addition to the social stigma it carried at the time, a diagnosis of HIV had broad implications for where patients could get treated or what type of health insurance was available to them. This had certainly been the case for Freddy. The next time he came in for a scheduled appointment, I ordered the HIV test to be repeated.

It returned a week later. Negative.

I called him to return and repeat the test, wanting to confirm the results before taking further action.

Again. Negative.

I called to tell him he had to keep his appointment, since I had something important to tell him.

"Freddy, you are not HIV positive."

"But you always told me that I was."

"Well, we have a new test, a better test. You were given a false positive, a mistake."

"You made a mistake?"

"Yes, I ordered the better test and it clarified the situation. It was a mistake, and I'm sorry. But the good news is that you are negative for HIV, and you never received unnecessary treatment for HIV while we thought you were positive. There was no inappropriate therapy." I thought that he should be happy about the news, but Freddy never got beyond his immediate wants.

Months later he requested his medical records, which is usually a sign of an impending malpractice lawsuit. He called me himself.

"I saw some people on Oprah, Doc. They all got money for being misdiagnosed as having AIDS."

"Freddy, you have to understand why I was slow to confirm the diagnosis. Your roommate had died from AIDS, you were having unprotected sex with dozens of partners, and you were sharing needles with other drug users."

"I never said those things," he said indignantly.

"Freddy, they're all in your chart."

"You wouldn't say that in court."

"Yes, that's how I would defend myself in court," I said, knowing that what I was saying was inappropriate and unprofessional.

"How about just sending me some money, Doc?"

"No, Freddy, no money."

I never saw Freddy again, and nothing came of his legal inquiry. About two years later I was told by a doctor who worked at a hospital in Kingsport that Freddy had come in with pneumonia, pneumocystis, a typical infection in patients with AIDS.

I regret the mistakes I made with Freddy's care. Even though his lifestyle was high-risk, I should not have waited so long to confirm his diagnosis, which affected his ability to get medical treatment elsewhere. And I should not have lost my patience when he came threatening me with a lawsuit. It was wrong of me to discuss the case with him the way I did, and I should have ended the conversation before it started. I allowed myself to get frustrated with Freddy's self-destructive behavior, and I think in the end it limited my ability to care for him. However, I tried to learn from mistakes and vowed to maintain my objectivity and professionalism in the face of frustrations in my future.

When my parents moved to Amarillo in 2001, I was glad to be close by to help take care of them. The move from Florida was particularly hard on my mother, and after her first cold winter in West Texas, she was ready for some tropical weather. We all agreed to go on a cruise to the Caribbean together that summer. However, a week before we were set to leave, my mom called to tell me that her back was bothering her. She told me that the pain began after she tried to move the couch in the living room. It sounded like a lumbosacral strain, the most typical cause of lower back pain. I told her that rest and heat would probably help resolve the problem in a few days.

The next day, my mom called to tell me that the pain was worse and that the hot pad had been too hot. It had burned the skin above her buttocks. She had taken over-the-counter pain medication, but it had not helped. I decided to call Mom's physician.

Dr. Jenkins was a former student of mine from East Tennessee, and now a faculty member at Texas Tech in Amarillo. She was an outstanding clinician who always said she learned her clinical skills from me. She claimed I taught her the importance of history and physical examination. I called to ask her to prescribe my mother stronger pain medication.

"Marjorie, Mom has low back pain. Do you mind writing a prescription for codeine to take with us on the cruise?"

"Have you examined her?" she asked.

"Well, she has limited range of motion after trying to move her couch."

"I'd like to see her before prescribing anything," Marjorie replied.

"Well, fine, but we leave in two days."

"That's okay; I'll make a home visit tonight."

We both arrived at my parents' home that night, and I waited in the living room while Dr. Jenkins performed the exam. She came to get me after five minutes.

"Steve, there's something I think you should see." We approached my mom together as she lay on her bed.

"My mother's behind?" I asked, surprised.

"No, come look."

There was a line of angry red blisters on my mother's lower back. I knew what it was immediately. Shingles! Even a medical student would recognize it, the wounds are so characteristic. Shingles, or zoster, is a virus related to chickenpox.

What a mistake! Wrong diagnosis. Wrong treatment. Wrong follow-up. I'm the infectious disease expert who wrote a paper on the management of shingles for geriatric journals! How could I have asked my former medical student, who respected my physical examination skills, to prescribe codeine for shingles? And for my own mother!

My mistakes were all classic reasons why physicians should not treat their own family members. I was distracted by our upcoming trip and did not take the time to perform an adequate examination. I assumed that the simplest explanation for her symptoms was correct and failed to ask questions that would have revealed that her pain was not musculoskeletal. I was glad that Dr. Jenkins was there to correct my mistakes, and I learned how important it was to have colleagues that I trusted to give my loved ones the best possible care.

I was heading with enthusiasm to see a recently admitted patient. My administrative duties at Tennessee had limited the amount of time I was spending in clinic, but I had been called specially for this case as an infectious disease consultant. By that point in my career, I had seen a lot of unusual and complicated cases, but there was still one problem that never failed to be an interesting challenge: the fever of unknown origin (FUO). By definition, a diagnosis of FUO means that a patient has had a fever for at least two weeks and no cause for the fever has been determined. That's when the infectious disease consultant is summoned. The residents had reached that point with Mr. Gagnon. As I approached the patient's room I reminded myself of the basics.

The causes of FUO are divided almost equally into three groups: true infections (either bacterial or viral), cancer, or inflammatory disease (such as lupus and arthritis). Often an unexplained fever is the result of a common disease presenting in an uncommon way. There are several usual suspects: tuberculosis and lymphoma are always possibilities. In every case, the most important clue to diagnosis is more likely to be something the patient tells you rather than the result of some laboratory test. If the history and physical lead nowhere, don't give up, keep searching. Gather information about the patient's pets, or recent travel to foreign places, exposure to uncooked foods or impure water, contact with family or friends who are sick. Eventually the answer will be revealed.

Mr. Gagnon did not look ill when he greeted me from his hospital bed. A young man in his twenties, he had thick glasses, dark hair, a medium build, and a friendly disposition. He turned off the TV and smiled at me. I jumped right in with a barrage of questions about his history and the course of his symptoms.

Mr. Gagnon was recently married, a lab technician struggling with a difficult job and erratic hours. He drank alcohol moderately, smoked a pack of cigarettes per day, and had recently lost his appetite. As best as he could tell, he had lost ten pounds over the past two weeks. For a month, he had been complaining of fever and occasional stomach pain, but he was suffering from no other symptoms.

I continued to pepper him with questions. Yes, he had a pet, a cat. No, he had not traveled outside of Tennessee in the past six months. His parents were of Italian descent. He did not take drugs. No, he couldn't think of anyone he'd come in contact with recently who was sick, but as a lab technician he did draw blood from patients. And sometimes he went to a nursing home to collect blood samples. But no, there had been no needle sticks, no open cuts or recent wounds.

I examined him and found that the lymph nodes in his neck were small but palpable. He had a soft heart murmur, but nothing serious. When I felt deeply in his abdomen, he complained of some pain. His mental status was completely normal. He was oriented, calm, and handling his illness well. "Just help me find out what's wrong so I can go back to work," he said.

The next step was to conduct blood tests and imaging. The results of both contained potential clues. Tests of his liver function were slightly abnormal, and his chest X-ray showed a slight shadow where the lung met the diaphragm.

I was anxious to find the cause of Mr. Gagnon's fever quickly. He seemed like he was in good health, but I was concerned about the recent weight loss. With FUO, weight loss sometimes precedes rapid decline and death. The stakes were high, and so I carefully considered all of the possibilities.

The shadow on his X-ray was a good lead: it could be tuberculosis presenting atypically without cough. He had been doing work in nursing homes where TB is quite common. Then again, hepatitis B or C were possible explanations for his slightly abnormal liver tests. Also, he did have some abdominal tenderness on physical examination, and with his Mediterranean background, it could be familial Mediterranean fever. Of course, he also had a cat, and I remembered his palpable lymph nodes: cat scratch fever was another possibility.

I returned to his bedside with another round of questions ready. Had his cat ever scratched him? Sure, all the time. Was there ever a history of fever and abdominal pain in his family? He wasn't sure, perhaps in his father. Had he ever drawn blood from a patient who was being treated for tuberculosis? Yes, on several occasions.

The morning after admission I was called by the nurse in charge. Mr. Gagnon's temperature was 102 degrees Fahrenheit, but his pulse, blood pressure, and respiratory rate were all normal. Pulse normally rises with temperature, but there are some diseases such as typhoid fever and leptospirosis where the pulse can remain normal. We had two more possible culprits for the fever.

As the workup proceeded, Mr. Gagnon's temperature stayed between 102 and 103. Lab tests were all normal except for his initial liver tests. We performed a CT scan of his abdomen, but nothing appeared abnormal. A skin test and sputum test both came back negative for tuberculosis, and there were no signs of any other infections in his blood and urine samples.

I sought out an experienced radiologist to review his chest X-ray.

"I suspect tuberculosis in Gagnon. He has had exposure." I pointed out the disturbing shadow, but the radiologist just smiled.

"You're overreading, again. He may have TB, but I'm not seeing it, and you're not either."

Every clue was a dead end. The patient continued to run a fever every morning, but there were no specific new findings on history or physical examination that could help us figure out what was wrong. Fortunately he had stopped losing weight in the hospital, and his vital signs—pulse, respiratory rate, and blood pressure—were all normal and stable. I suggested additional tests: an ultrasound of the heart to evaluate his mild heart murmur. I also considered doing a biopsy of a lymph node in his neck. When I suggested it to Mr. Gagnon, he was agreeable to the idea.

"Just do whatever has to be done to figure this out."

Blood tests returned normal, and we ruled out cat scratch fever, typhoid fever, and leptospirosis. Tests for hepatitis B and C were negative, and in fact his abnormal liver function tests returned to normal after a second round of testing. We measured his erythrocyte sedimentation rate, which indicates the amount of inflammation in the body. The test results are almost always elevated in a patient with fever of unknown origin, but they were completely normal. A week had gone by, and all our leads had led nowhere.

The patient's primary care physician was a young family medicine doctor, trained to know disease, but also to know his patient. We met in the hospital cafeteria to exchange notes, and he surprised me with his diagnosis.

"I don't think there's anything wrong with him—he needs to go home."

I thought perhaps he was just discouraged by our failed attempts to diagnose the problem. "FUO is a tough diagnosis and requires patience," I suggested.

"No, there's nothing wrong with him," my colleague insisted.

I thought about it. The patient did appear to be in good health. He had complained of weight loss, but he had not lost a pound in the hospital. I reconsidered his other symptoms. His initial liver function tests were definitely a concern, but now they were back to normal, perhaps because he had not had anything alcoholic to drink during his week in the hospital. There was that abnormal chest X-ray. But that was nothing according to the radiologist. And lots of people have Italian heritage but not familial Mediterranean fever. And every cat owner gets scratched every once in a while. The only thing left was fever. Just fever, and only in the morning, and not with an accompanying rise in pulse or elevated erythrocyte sedimentation rate.

Suddenly, I realized what the problem was. How could I have missed this diagnosis for so long? The statistic is mentioned in every paper ever published on FUO: 9 percent of all cases are factitious fever, a fever, or temperature, induced by the patient. I couldn't believe it. Mr. Gagnon seemed so normal, so happy and cooperative. But it was the only diagnosis that fit.

The rest of the case was handled by the primary care physician in consultation with the hospital attorney. Mr. Gagnon's nightstand was searched, and a hot pad and two thermometers were found. The nursing staff confirmed that sometimes he had refused to cooperate with the normal temperature-taking procedures. When confronted, he admitted to raising the recorded temperature of the thermometer by several different means: hot pad, radiator, his morning cup of tea. He declined psychiatric evaluation and left the hospital. I never heard about him again.

I had missed the diagnosis because I thought Mr. Gagnon was too well adjusted to fake an illness. I was too trusting and assumed his symptoms were legitimate. His case was a reminder of how unpredictable medicine can be. It taught me that despite my years of experience, there was still much more for me to see and learn.

In 1988, Mr. Montaigne came to the emergency room in Tennessee complaining of fever, fatigue, poor appetite, and weight loss. He had been to both the ER and the clinic four or five times in the past three weeks. The resident who saw him called me down to examine him, since he had been to the hospital repeatedly without showing signs of improvement.

"Dr. Berk. We want you to see a patient in the emergency room. He isn't really that sick, but his white count is elevated. He says he's been sick for a month and still isn't feeling better."

I went down to the emergency room and recognized the patient right away. He was already a close acquaintance, a friend. Mr. Montaigne was tall and lanky, with thick glasses and neatly trimmed hair that always looked like he had just been to the barber. That day he was wearing a green flannel shirt that seemed too large for him. He smiled when he saw me, revealing a missing front tooth.

"I don't feel right, Dr. Berk," he told me. "I'm always tired. I have no energy. Every day is a struggle. They gave me a prescription, and after I took them I felt better for a little while. But now I'm right back where I started."

I examined the patient carefully. I must have been more thorough than previous examiners, because I noticed several signs that were not mentioned in his chart. He had tiny pinpoint red dots on his lower eyelids, and there were red lines on his fingernails, just above the nail beds. The sound of his heart was abnormal; I could hear a murmur in between the "lub dub" sounds made by valves closing in his heart. I felt his spleen and found that it was enlarged.

The diagnosis was clear: it was endocarditis, an infection of the heart. The round of antibiotics Mr. Montaigne was prescribed had helped his symptoms briefly, but it was the wrong prescription at the wrong dose. The diagnosis had been delayed for weeks, and the infection persisted. But now we had a diagnosis and could find the proper treatment.

We carefully cultured Mr. Montaigne's blood to isolate the bacteria causing his infection and determine the proper antibiotic to treat it. In cases of endocarditis, antibiotics must be administered at very high doses by an intravenous line. A full course should be delivered carefully over six weeks. In Mr. Montaigne's case, the bacteria was difficult to identify, but after two days we found the culprit, and I prescribed an aggressive regimen of penicillin and rifampin.

Over the next three weeks, Mr. Montaigne's condition improved steadily. After four weeks on antibiotics, he told me he was feeling better than he had in a year. He and his wife were astounded and incredibly grateful, and I felt like a hero. I was the physician who figured out what was wrong when others had missed the diagnosis.

During his fifth week in the hospital, Mr. Montaigne developed a blood clot in his leg. The condition is called deep vein phlebitis, and it is a common complication in patients who have spent a long time immobilized in a hospital bed. Phlebitis is usually treated with the blood thinner Coumadin. The dose of the drug must be carefully calibrated for each patient, and so every day we measured Mr. Montaigne's prothrombin time (PT). The PT level is a measure of how quickly it takes the blood to clot. If it is too low, there is risk of developing another phlebitis. If it is high, the patient can suffer from internal bleeding. By the time we found the right dose for Mr. Montaigne, he was ready to be discharged. His antibiotic regimen was finally finished, and he went home feeling much healthier than when he had arrived.

But his good health did not last. About a week later, I was called by a physician on duty in the intensive care unit. Mr. Montaigne had just been admitted for a very serious stroke. I told him to order a CT scan to check for blood on the brain, and he called me back quickly to confirm that there was indeed a bad bleed into Mr. Montaigne's brain.

"And the PT level?" I asked.

"Abnormal." It was high. Too high. Sky high.

I went in to see the patient right away, but by the time I arrived he was already coding. His heart had stopped beating; he had stopped breathing. Physicians and nurses attempted resuscitation, but it was too late. He was dead.

Shocked and saddened, I reviewed the case. His PT was too high, his blood was thin, and he had a bad bleed into the brain. It looked like an overdose of Coumadin, but I was sure Mr. Montaigne could be relied on to take his medication according to the prescription. I took a look at his charts to check his PT level at discharge: it was perfectly normal. I looked for the date his antibiotics were stopped: penicillin and rifampin were stopped after a six-week course.

There was the answer: rifampin. The antibiotic inhibits Coumadin. When it was stopped, the Coumadin became too strong, making Mr. Montaigne's blood dangerously thin and causing the bleed into his brain. It was something the resident who discharged Mr. Montaigne would not have known. I should have recalibrated his Coumadin dose myself after he went off the rifampin. He had died from a drug interaction, a medical error. The patient that I had saved from endocarditis was dead because of a mistake I made in his prescription.

Mr. Montaigne's death was a painful reminder of my imperfection. I thought he was cruising to a successful recovery, and so I missed a key detail that led to his stroke. It was a fatal mistake, and one that I will regret for the rest of my life. The only thing I could do after making such a huge error was to take responsibility for it and to learn from it. I would not make the same mistake again. I would be more attentive, more careful, more diligent. It was the only way for me to respond to a mistake of that magnitude. I did my best to grow from the experience and be a better physician because of it.

• • •

So I have made my share of mistakes in life. Some have been small hiccups and faux pas, embarrassing moments that I cringe to remember. Others have been errors that haunt me to this day. But with every mistake, I have tried to take responsibility for my actions, to learn from what I did wrong, and to make amends when I can.

I glance at the man sitting next to me, speeding through Bushland, Texas. Beside him are a shotgun, a kidnapped doctor, and a jewelry drawer full of stolen rings. He has robbed me, abducted me, and threatened to kill me. But he says it is not his fault.

"I was pushed into this by some mistakes," he tells me.

Perhaps it's true. We all make mistakes, and I know that even small errors can have unforeseen consequences that extend beyond our control. I feel hesitantly sympathetic toward this man. I wonder what kind of massive mistakes have brought him to this desperate point. Whatever they are, they have ruined his life. I wonder if his next mistake will ruin mine.

8

Leslie

M eadow, Texas, is a town of 658 people and 213 house-
holds. The name is pronounced *MED-uh*, but only by
the local townsfolk, who live scattered on their farms
and ranches, isolated one from another by acres of flat land. Perhaps Meadow's name was more fitting when the town was found-
ed in 1904, when the land was still mostly grassland used to graze
huge herds of cattle. Now, the land around Meadow is composed
of dry agricultural fields and low-lying brush.

I have never been to Meadow, but in 2005, Leslie J. had lived
there for thirty-three years. Actually she lived on a quiet country
road just outside of the city limits; her nearest neighbor was a
mile down the road. On a weekday afternoon on a cool, clear day
in March, Leslie came home from work in town to find an unfamiliar car in her driveway. It was a white SUV, a Montero Sport,
with the "N" of Montero missing from the side. Surprised, she
was reluctant to go into her house. She knew her husband was at
a Lions Club meeting, and she was not expecting company. That

morning Leslie had left her cell phone at home, and she had only come back to the house to pick it up before heading out to run an errand. Unable to call her husband, and unsure of what to do, Leslie waited in her car for twenty minutes before deciding to enter the house, grab her cell phone, and leave.

She approached the side door of her house uneasily. As she reached for the doorknob, a man burst out at her with a gun. He pointed a rifle at her head and pushed her into the house.

The intruder was wearing black panty hose over his face and black socks on his hands. While his features were barely visible, Leslie could see that he was a white male with fair skin. His hairy eyebrows showed through the panty hose mask.

He asked her if she had called anyone while she was waiting in the car. She responded that she did not have her cell phone. Still pointing the gun at her, he asked for cash and became agitated when she said she had none. He demanded her purse. She told him it was still in her car. As she brushed past him to get to the garage, she shuddered and cringed.

"I'm a druggie, not a rapist," he told her with aggravation. "I want you to get the purse. Just don't make me kill you."

Leslie retrieved her purse from the car and returned to the kitchen, where the gunman quickly rummaged through it, taking cash and credit cards from her wallet. He asked for jewelry, but she had nothing else of value in the house.

As the stranger robbed her, Leslie noticed that her husband's gun cabinet was open and empty.

The gunman followed her gaze and asked, "What time is your husband coming home, Leslie?" He learned her name from the credit cards and used it menacingly now.

"I don't know," she replied.

"You better hope that he doesn't."

The gunman looked out the kitchen window at a swing set and playground in the backyard.

"I'm sure you have grandchildren that play out there," he told her. "I can come back here and kill them. I can kill you and your family. Or have friends sent back to kill you."

Convinced that there was nothing else for him to take, the intruder loaded the stolen guns and reached into his pocket to pull out Leslie's cell phone. He wiped it clean and handed it to her.

"I'm going to give this back to you," he said. "But you can never tell anyone what happened here. You can't tell your husband, and you better never call the police. Because if you do, Leslie, I will kill you. And I will come back here and kill your family." He asked her for a family picture. Speechless, she motioned toward a picture of her and her grandchildren on the refrigerator, which he grabbed and stuffed into his pocket.

"I know what your family looks like, and I will kill those babies. Do you have a land line?"

"Yes."

"I have a scanner, and so I'll know if you call the police."

She did not reply.

"What time is it?" he asked.

"12:25."

"You sit there till 12:30 and don't get up or I'll kill you."

He walked out the door, but returned two minutes later.

She had not moved, frozen in fear.

He scowled and said, "Good job, Leslie," then left again.

She stayed seated and trembling at the kitchen table. She was afraid to use her telephone, afraid to move but also afraid to stay in her home. Fifteen minutes later, she left the house and drove straight to her husband's Lions Club meeting.

State of Texas v. Jack Lindsey Jordan

DISTRICT ATTORNEY EVANS: After you went and found your husband, did you decide to call law enforcement?

LESLIE: I didn't want to.

EVANS: Why, Leslie?

LESLIE: Because the first thing I said is, I guess I wasn't thinking straight, but all [I] can remember is just him telling me over and over that he'll kill [me] and [my] family if [I] call anybody. So I wasn't thinking straight and just kept saying [to my husband], please don't call anybody.

EVANS: Did you finally get over your fear and make the decision to call?

LESLIE: I guess Lloyd made that decision for me.

EVANS: Okay, Leslie. Has this affected your life, this incident?

LESLIE: You'll never know what it is like not to be able to just feel good about going home. Because I still don't. Every day when I drive into that driveway or when I'm in that garage, I still remember, and I hope and pray that it will fade. But it is not fun when home is not a safe place.

EVANS: Do you still have problems sleeping?

LESLIE: Yes ma'am.

EVANS: Do you have concerns and fears about your family?

LESLIE: Yes ma'am.

EVANS: What kind of fears?

LESLIE: I didn't want my kids or grandkids coming out there. I pleaded with them; please don't come to the house anymore. I didn't want them there. I didn't think it was a safe place.

EVANS: In state exhibit 14, what do you recognize that photo to be?

LESLIE: It's a white Montero Sport with an N missing from the Montero.

. . .

DISTRICT ATTORNEY EVANS: On March 5 did you at some point during your meeting get notified by your wife that something had happened?

LLOYD: Yes, I was sitting in the meeting. From where I was sitting I could see the front door, and I saw her come in. I immediately knew that something was wrong, so I got up and went to talk to her.

EVANS: What was her demeanor? What was she acting like?

LLOYD: She was very upset and told me that a man was in our house when she went home and held her at gunpoint. I immediately told the secretary to call 911, and she got really upset then and said he threatened to kill me and all our family and grandchildren if she told the police or told me. And so she was very upset, but I knew that is all we could do.

EVANS: So she was terrified—she was trying to stop you from calling.

LLOYD: Yes.

EVANS: Lloyd, did this incident have an effect on your wife?

LLOYD: Definitely.

EVANS: How has it affected her?

LLOYD: It's been tough. I have to pick her up from lunch every day. She still hasn't come in or out of the doors that he came out of. She won't stay home by herself. You know we live out in the country. We have talked about moving. She is always leery of any car that drives up. Just, you know, she has been terrorized. It's changed our lives. We have an alarm system. We lock doors that we didn't use to. We don't have that peace anymore in our own home.

. . .

DISTRICT ATTORNEY BLOUNT: Mr. Jordan, is it your position that you did not rob or burglarize the house of Leslie and Lloyd?

JORDAN: Absolutely, I did not.

BLOUNT: Have you ever met those people before?

JORDAN: No, I have never seen them before.

BLOUNT: They have no reason, then, to dislike you or have a grudge against you.

JORDAN: No.

BLOUNT: Would you agree that Leslie had no reason to say that the assailant's vehicle was a white Montero missing an N just like yours?

JORDAN: No.

BLOUNT: Would you agree with me that Lloyd had no reason to come in here and say that your weapons were the ones that were taken from his home?

JORDAN: No sir, absolutely not.

BLOUNT: Would you agree with me that it is awfully coincidental that an assailant driving a white Mitsubishi Montero with a missing "N" robs Leslie on March 5, a day before you go into Dr. Berk's residence, and ends up with a rifle and a 20-gauge shotgun and shells that appear for all the world to be the ones taken on March 5?

JORDAN: Yes sir.

BLOUNT: You agree that that's an awfully big coincidence?

JORDAN: I think that's an extreme coincidence.

9

Shame in Bushland

had been to Bushland only once before in my life. It was when a close family friend visited us in Amarillo and brought Justin a telescope as a gift. Justin was interested in astronomy at the time, and so we all drove out to a cattle ranch in Bushland to go stargazing and try out the new telescope. It was the perfect place for such a trip: the evening was dark, clear, and perfectly quiet. There was no man-made light for miles around, and nothing to distract us from the awesome magnificence of the starlit sky.

Bushland has a post office, a mercantile store, and an ancient grain elevator that has been there since the Great Depression, when the population of Bushland was still only about twenty. Today, as my kidnapper speeds his SUV into town, there are 430 residents living in Bushland, but none of them appears to be on the road with us.

We enter the small town and find the type of gas station that the gunman has been looking for all day. The pumps are far from the pay station and there isn't another customer in sight. He stares at me as he fills up the tank. I sit very still in the passenger seat, knowing that with a full tank of gas and easy access to the interstate, we are at a crossroads. I cannot predict what he will do with me. He can leave me here or let me out of the car somewhere down the road. Or he can drive me farther out into the country and kill me or abandon me in a field. I consider getting out of the car and running toward the pay station, but he's watching me carefully and I decide against it.

State of Texas v. Jack Lindsey Jordan

DISTRICT ATTORNEY BLOUNT: There came a point when you and the defendant were in Bushland, and he was outside the vehicle pumping gas, and you were still in the vehicle.

BERK: That's true.

BLOUNT: Why at that point did you not try to run?

BERK: Well, first of all, if you see where the gas station is, there is nothing to run to. There's just open road. And I mean seven seconds later I would just be fifty yards away. Plus as I said, I thought it was winding down, that I had a good chance that he would take I-40 and let me go.

BLOUNT: Was there a point you felt you had the opportunity to take the weapon?

BERK: I had thought many times about grabbing the weapon, and actually the feeling you have is that that is the best thing to do. But rationally I said that it was not a good idea. I mean if I was more skilled with guns that might have been more of an option.

BLOUNT: Do you have any military training?

BERK: No.

BLOUNT: Any law enforcement training?

BERK: No.

BLOUNT: Any combat training?
BERK: No.

He uses my credit card to pay for the gas and gets back in the car. He drives under the interstate, turns left on the frontage road, and then pulls off of the pavement to park the car in an isolated field. We are less than half a mile from the gas station, but the area is completely deserted. This is the critical moment. It is clear that he does not want to take me with him on I-40, so there are really only two options left. He can kill me out here by the side of the road, or he can let me go and drive away.

Shooting me here is perhaps his best option. There is no one else around, and no one in Amarillo even knows that I'm gone yet. He can kill me, hide my body, and flee. Perhaps it will never be found. And even if it is, there is no real trail connecting me to him; he has left no trail in Amarillo, there are no fingerprints in my home, and no one in town has seen him or his vehicle. He used my credit card twice to buy gas, but neither station had a video camera. No, I'm the only thing that can link him to his crime. If he kills me here, he is much less likely to get caught.

I look out into the surrounding fields and wonder if this is it.

"Remember, I know where you live, and I would kill you," says the kidnapper.

He gives me back my wallet, my wife's wallet, and my garage door opener. (I don't notice at the time, but he keeps my credit cards.) With this gesture, he gives me back my life.

I nod in appreciation and put my hand on the handle of the passenger door. All this time, I have been imagining the different ways I might escape that SUV through that door. I envisioned myself making a desperate leap from the moving vehicle or a mad dash from the car while it was stalled at a traffic light. But no, all I have to do is open the door and get out of the car. When

I turn the handle; the door swings open with ease. The gunman does not stop me, but before I get out of the car, he asks a question.

"Where does this highway go if I take it east?"

"To Oklahoma City," I tell him.

He scowls slightly. "How about west?"

"New Mexico."

"I prefer New Mexico," he tells me quietly.

Inexplicably, before I climb out of the SUV, we exchange a fist bump. It is like a modern-day handshake, bumping the knuckles of our clenched fists together, something my sons have taught me. Without another word, I get out of the vehicle and shut the door behind me. He puts the car in gear and pulls back onto the access road.

State of Texas v. Jack Lindsey Jordan

DISTRICT ATTORNEY BLOUNT: If you would tell us what happened as you and Mr. Jordan left each other that day?

BERK: We got gas, we moved to the other side of 40. We were in a pretty secluded spot. He tells me again, reminds me that if I were to tell anyone what happened he would kill me and my family. And that is it. And I start opening the door and he's obviously going to let me out.

BLOUNT: And that is when the fist bumping occurred?

BERK: Yes.

BLOUNT: And, okay, why did you do that?

BERK: I guess it was just what they do. I don't know. It was just what they do I guess.

BLOUNT: And okay, who was the first one to initiate the fist bump?

BERK: I think it was him.

BLOUNT: Okay.

BERK: I mean, I do that with my kids. But I think it was him. I
  can't remember for sure.

I watch him drive away and briefly contemplate the strange ordeal that I've been through, which I hope is finally over. I think
about this enigmatic man and the strange conclusion of our interactions on that Sunday afternoon.

Why did he let me go? He set me free even though it was probably not in his best interest. He must know that what he did constitutes aggravated kidnapping, a crime that carries the maximum penalty of life in prison. Killing me was probably his best
bet for avoiding a life sentence. Why did he let me live? Perhaps
he felt some level of human compassion. He didn't think of himself as a murderer, and I learned later that he had never killed
anyone in cold blood. Or maybe he respected me as a physician.
And perhaps he felt that I had treated him with respect in return.
Whatever the reason, I'm extremely grateful that he let me go,
grateful that he could have killed me but chose not to do so. Perhaps I will always be more grateful than angry.

I wonder what our fist bump meant. I don't understand what
he expected from me. He kidnapped me and threatened to kill
me and my family. His parting words were that he knew where I
lived. He clearly wanted me to remain silent about his crime out
of fear of retribution. It was an act of intimidation that he had
probably used with victims before. So why the fist bump?

And why did he open up about his personal history? The story
about his wife's death and the date of his surgery could be used
to identify him. But he seemed to share that information freely.
He shed tears over his wife in my presence, while he was committing a serious crime. And he just now told me he was heading

for New Mexico. This man drove down the residential streets of Amarillo looking behind us at every turn, but now he tells me the next stop he has planned on his road trip?

Does he think I'm his doctor? Does he know the Hippocratic Oath, and its vow of confidentiality? Does he know the words I swore upon becoming a physician, that "What I may see and hear in the course of treatment in regard to the life of men I will keep to myself, holding such things shameful to be spoken about." Or does he just have high expectations for the behavior of others?

Standing on the side of the road at the edge of an empty field, I wonder at the riddles this man has left me, at the strange quirks of human nature and the odd and terrifying events that I have just survived.

And then I think, *Scream. Scream both to call for help and to celebrate your life.*

But I do not scream.

Run, run for safety. I realize that I may still be in danger. The gunman could easily change his mind and return. I begin to run down a small dirt road, avoiding the highway because I think it will be easier for him to find me there if he decides to come back. About a half mile down the road, I see a grain elevator, its white cylinders rising up over wooden sheds painted powder blue. There, at the intersection of West Twentieth Street and SRM 2338, I stop and wait for someone to help me.

Several cars pass, but no one even slows down as I wave frantically from the side of the road. I can see their faces as they pass. One man looks at his watch. He must be late for an appointment. Another woman looks fearful, and speeds up as she passes me by. A third driver is annoyed as I move closer to the middle of the road. The fourth one pretends not to see me at all.

I become more aggressive, flagging down cars from the middle of the street and even pleading for someone to stop with my hands together in supplication. Now the faces look even more disapproving. *Shame on you,* the drivers are thinking. Yes, that is the word, that is the feeling. There is no joy in freedom at this moment. Only shame.

I am not dressed appropriately: I'm wearing a Houston Texans T-shirt, shorts, no socks, and sneakers. I did not get a chance to shave this morning, and my hair looks wild in the West Texas wind that is blowing across the panhandle. I am definitely underdressed.

It was the mid-1970s, and I had flown from Boston to New Jersey to visit my parents and to attend a conference in New York. I was leaving the house to take a bus to Manhattan where Dr. Jonas Salk was giving a speech. Salk was my idol, an infectious disease physician who made one of the most outstanding discoveries of all time: the polio vaccine. As I was leaving the house, my mother critiqued my appearance.

"Steve, your hair is too long, and that corduroy jacket is too old. And those shoes, Steve. What are you wearing on your feet? You're going to meet Jonas Salk in those shoes?" I was wearing Wallabees, a brand of shoes that was popular among college students at the time.

I left the house without changing, but as I walked from the bus station to the hotel where Salk was scheduled to speak, I began to agree with my mom. I looked like a college student. Salk was a great man, a famous physician. Perhaps I should have dressed more respectfully: a black suit, a neatly pressed button-down shirt, and black polished shoes.

I entered the hotel conference room and confirmed my worst

fears. The room held a small audience of about a hundred expectant dignified men and women, all dressed in black suits. I joined the crowd a bit sheepishly, and we all waited for the guest of honor.

Shortly, Jonas Salk himself came in and shook hands with everyone in the room. He had a great presence, and I think we were all impressed with his distinguished demeanor. As he approached to shake my hand, I noticed that, despite his balding, he kept his hair long in the back. It was quite long actually, and he was wearing a corduroy jacket. I glanced down as he shook my hand. Yes, Wallabee shoes.

I smiled with relief and awe as I shook the hand of this medical pioneer. He went up to the podium to deliver his lecture, and I sat in the audience wiggling my toes in my Wallabees.

In Bushland, more cars speed past, and I imagine how they must see me. *You do not understand,* I want to tell them. *I am not a vagabond. I'm not what you think.*

In the winter of 1969, I was standing at a bus station near the Fernald School for the mentally disabled, just down the road from Brandeis University in Waltham, Massachusetts. That Saturday morning I was volunteering at the Fernald School, and my assignment was to take a small group of the handicapped residents on a shopping trip to Boston. The trip was supposed to be a learning experience for the four mentally handicapped adults who were traveling with me. They had been earning minimum wage for doing jobs at the school, and I was supposed to help them use, manage, and value the money they had saved. I would teach them how much a hamburger cost or help them pay for a ticket to see *Butch Cassidy and the Sundance Kid*. On the way home, we would decide whether to take the bus or a taxi and compare the difference in cost.

As we waited for the bus to arrive, my charges were excited but not unruly. Nonetheless, our group was drawing attention from passersby. Many mentally challenged individuals have genetic abnormalities that affect their facial features: they have long faces, or big ears, wide eyes, short stature. It was not strange for some people to notice our unusual group.

After about five minutes, a Waltham policeman stopped by to say hello. Perhaps he was regularly assigned to the area around the school, because he did not seem to find anything unusual about our group waiting at the bus stop.

"Where are you boys going today?" he addressed us all cheerfully.

"To the mooo-vies," said one.

"To get popcorn," said another enthusiastically.

The policeman turned to me. He got close to my face and said, "I bet you like popcorn too!"

"I do," I told him, not knowing what else to say.

"And you need to zip up your jacket or you'll catch cold, big fella." I was wearing an unzipped leather jacket over a heavy winter sweater.

I did not know how to respond. I considered saying, "Sir, I am not a member of the Fernald School as you have assumed." But I chose not to respond. The officer left and the bus arrived shortly after.

Stranded and helpless at this intersection in Bushland, Texas, I feel a disheartening sense of shame. I join other victims of crime who have felt disgraced and humiliated for being a part of a crime for which they were not responsible. As a physician, I have seen this shame in others. I remember the first rape victim I saw in the emergency room. I did not know how to help her with the overwhelming shame she felt that night. No training had prepared me to help her overcome such a difficult emotion. I remember the woman who came in battered and bleeding because of her abusive husband. She could not even tell us what had happened, and she could barely answer yes-or-no questions. I remember the stripper who came to the emergency room in her G-string and sequined bra. She had a knife sticking out of her back, put there by a jealous rival while she was dancing onstage. The shame of that crime was almost contagious, for even I felt a sense of embarrassment in being distantly involved in whatever situation had led to such a gruesome injury.

Standing at the intersection of West Twentieth Street and SRM 2338, I suddenly understand what those patients must have felt. I remember their pitiful expressions, and I feel sorry for them and for myself too.

State of Texas v. Jack Lindsey Jordan

DEFENSE ATTORNEY BAILEY, Closing Argument:
Because if you recall, when he is talking to his family everything is fine. He sends his son off to church, no problem. Goes back in smiling to his wife. Everything seemed to be fine with her, and yet supposedly he took a man who was threatening to kill him back home to his wife. And if you want to find that believable, a man who was sitting there threatening to kill you gets out of the vehicle, goes back and pumps gas.

It happens all the time: shame the victim in order to defend the criminal. The girl who was raped wore a short skirt. The battered wife should have left her husband years ago. Why did she even marry him in the first place? That stripper surrounded herself with the dregs of society. She had it coming. And the kidnapped doctor? Well, he took a gunman home to his wife, and he didn't run when he got the chance.

Perhaps I am guilty of the crime committed against me.

Yes, I left my garage door open.

I did not wrestle the gun from my captor or jump from the car.

I got myself stranded, with no money and no phone.

And I am not properly dressed for a Sunday afternoon.

I can tell that I am annoying the people of Bushland with my antics in the street.

A nearby road sign informs me that, "This road was a gift of the Bushland Baptist Church." I think bitterly that I am unable to get help on a Sunday afternoon from men and women who are probably returning from church. But to them, I am not a victim. I am just a strange and wild-looking man in the middle of the street.

After about fifteen cars and another fifteen minutes pass, a middle-aged woman and her daughter stop their station wagon for me and let me use their cell phone.

I dial Shirley's number but mistakenly get my son Jeremy, whose phone number is only one digit away from my wife's. I regret the error and try to get off the phone as quickly as possible.

"I've just been kidnapped. I'll get right back to you."

That was so stupid, I think to myself. But I hang up and call my wife. I don't realize at the time that Jeremy was already worried about me, even before that frantic, cryptic call.

I get in touch with Shirley. "I was kidnapped at gunpoint," I tell her. My voice is drained and emotionless, and I'm too distracted to notice how she reacts. I'm completely detached from the situation. I'm just reporting what has happened: A kidnapping has occurred. I was the person kidnapped.

Silence. She must be surprised. It's only 12:30 in the afternoon, and she has not yet begun to miss me.

"Pick me up. I'm in Bushland, off Interstate 40. I'm considering whether or not to call the police. And please bring a sweatshirt; I'm so cold."

"You must be kidding, Steve. Of course you should call the police."

To everyone else, perhaps it seems obvious that the first thing I should do is call law enforcement. The crime should be reported, the criminal pursued, and—hopefully—further crime prevented. But I understand why some people do not call the police. Right now, my ordeal is over. Getting the cops involved means reliving the crime, prolonging it, and bringing it home again for my family to deal with. It also means going public, perhaps risking more shame. I don't want to become known as a crime victim. I like my current reputation as physician and dean, and I would prefer to move on and leave this all behind me.

Moreover, I believe my kidnapper is capable of revenge, and I worry about his threats to return. I know him: he is unpredictable and dangerous, and I'm still afraid of him.

"Well, I'm not sure. It's something I want to think about. He did let me go."

After getting off the phone with Shirley, I realize that I cannot avoid getting the police involved. My kidnapper will just continue his crime spree if I don't report him, and perhaps by saying something I can help prevent future victims. Yes, remaining silent would be a mistake. I dial 911 on the borrowed cell phone and tell the operator that I have been kidnapped and stranded in Bushland. She asks for my location and tells me that officers are on their way. Finished with my phone calls, I return the cell phone to the woman who has been waiting with her daughter by the roadside. They have been gracious and kind, but they do not want to wait with me for the police to come. I understand and tell them thank you for their help.

I wait for the Potter County police to pick me up at the Bushland Mercantile, a country store set back from the intersection where I was trying to flag people down. The shop is closed, but for some reason I feel safe sitting there on a bench under its green awning. I sigh and wait. Minutes later, I begin shaking, only partially from the cold.

State of Texas v. Jack Lindsey Jordan

> DISTRICT ATTORNEY EVANS: When you first encountered him [Dr. Berk], did you find out from him what happened?
>
> DEPUTY WAGNER: Yes, I did.
>
> EVANS: And what did you find out?
>
> WAGNER: Basically he told me that he had been kidnapped from his residence at gunpoint and dropped off at that location.
>
> EVANS: What was his emotional state when you found him there?
>
> WAGNER: When I approached him he was visibly upset. He

was shaking. He was taking quick breaths. And talking fast
like he was scared or adrenaline was pumping.

Shirley arrives at the store a few minutes after the Potter County
police officer. She has brought an old red and white Boston U
sweatshirt, a relic from medical school. I put it on gratefully and
my shivering subsides. I begin to tell my story to Shirley and the
officer. He asks me where I was let out of the car and goes back
to examine the site, checking for tire tracks. Shortly, however, he
tells us to go home. Officers from the Randall County police force
will meet me at my house and conduct the main investigation
there. The kidnapping had occurred in Amarillo, in Randall
County, and so technically we were out of Bushland jurisdiction.
I'm grateful to be going home.

Shirley drives us back to Amarillo along Interstate 40. I call
Justin from her cell phone to make sure he is safe and to let him
know what has happened. Most of all, I want to tell him not to go
home. I'm still scared that the gunman will return, and I don't
want Justin in the house alone.

"Justin, we had a crime in our house. Don't go home quite
yet."

"Why, Dad?"

"Well, the guy said that he would come back. I just don't want
you home before we come home."

"I'll stay at Brandon's house."

"Yes, that's fine. I'll call you later."

"You sounded upset when you said good-bye, like you had gotten some bad news."

"I'll tell you all about it later."

I hang up and take a deep breath. I look out the window and
watch the familiar Amarillo landscape stream by. We pass Cadil-

lac Ranch, a line of ten graffiti-covered Cadillac cars buried nose-down in a cow pasture along the side of I-40, a monument of sorts and a famous hallmark of Amarillo. I've never thought much of the sculpture, but today it looks wonderful to me. It means I'm going home. As we enter Amarillo, I see the School of Medicine building in the distance to the left. It looks majestic against the blue sky. It is a brand-new building that I helped design, and in that moment it represents all the good things in my life. I look out at that building and feel grateful to be alive.

10

Amarillo Police

A marillo police cars are parked along the curb parallel to our home, and eventually the line stretches down the street. They draw attention from our neighbors, who have never seen so many squad cars gathered in a place without a car wreck nearby. The police are creating a traffic jam, taking up parking spaces that are usually occupied by soccer moms and dads attending the weekend games at the school down the street. In our neighborhood, the quiet of Sunday morning is typically replaced by the chaos of Sunday afternoon: every week we hear the parental hollering, cussing, and referee baiting as five-year-olds scamper hesitantly back and forth across the fields.

As policemen enter the house, mostly in pairs, they remind me of an internal medicine team gathering to make rounds with the special enthusiasm and skepticism reserved for an unusual case. They have their uniforms, emblems, and equipment, as we do. They all look the same with their neat black shirts, top button buttoned, and crisp black trousers. They all have the same impressive emblem on the right shoulder: an embroidered badge of red, gold, and brown that says POLICE in black letters across the top. They each have a silver badge gleaming on the left chest and a name badge on the right side, sometimes accompanied by other medals or recognition. Their black belts sag with the weight of their holsters and their large, prominent revolvers. One or two cell phones also hang from each belt in addition to some nightsticks. One patrolman has a walkie-talkie hanging from his shoulder as well. They are well equipped to communicate.

They chatter among themselves, respecting a particular hierarchy that determines who will speak and when. A trainee is particularly friendly and sympathetic toward me, but I can tell he's not very high in the pecking order, and I'm reminded of being a medical student at the bedside of a patient with unusual complications. I had very little to offer, but I wanted to be involved in whatever way I could. I realize suddenly that my kidnapping is like the case of a patient with an incredible story, an amazing array of symptoms, but no findings on physical examination. Even the veteran policemen are interested in the strange story: the brazen home invasion, the son's escape, the kidnapping at gunpoint, failed ATM visit, return to the scene with wife at home, and the sorrowful perpetrator who shared his life story before setting his captive free. But there are no bruises or gunshot wounds to the victim, no bullet holes in the walls of the house, no broken-down doors, no stolen cars or missing safes, no hysterical family members. Yes, the patient has interesting symptoms, but there are no clues as to what the diagnosis might be.

At one point, I overhear an officer mention that the last kidnapping that was reported in Amarillo was several years ago. It turned out to be faked: the victim had made everything up. I recognize the skepticism that is a healthy component of any early investigation. But I need them to believe me. I tell them that I'm the dean of the medical school. In fact, I've been working to help the local police force on a project with the district attorney. We're trying to bring a forensic pathologist to Amarillo so that the force will no longer have to outsource their autopsies to Lubbock every time there's a homicide. They respect my position and listen carefully to my story, but my recent sense of shame and my inability to give them more information puts me on the defensive.

Justin, Shirley, and I tell our stories separately and simultaneously. I think of the law shows I have seen, where the suspects are being interrogated at the same time in different rooms. But instead of the dark, mirrored rooms I've seen on TV, we use the living room, the dining room, and the kitchen. I sit across from two officers at my kitchen table, doing my best to answer their questions as fully as possible.

I believe I'm the only person who has seen the perpetrator, though perhaps someone saw us when we were driving around. The streets were deserted.

No, he did not leave anything in our house, and I don't know if he touched anything while he was here.

No, I did not know who he was. I had never seen him before.

We went to an ATM, but no, I don't think it had surveillance cameras.

No, he never hit me. I don't have any injuries.

"What was the make of the car?" asks the policeman, looking down at the notes he has written so far.

"I'm not sure. An SUV, a white SUV."

"Wasn't the make of the car on the steering wheel?"

No, I didn't think so. But there were the letters SPS.

The officer shakes his head. "That just means the car had power steering. So you don't know what type of car it was, even though you were in it for a very long time?"

"No, I don't know the make of the car," I reply dejectedly. The interview is going nowhere.

Then I remember. "Oh! But I do know the vehicle registration number."

I've known many answers in my career—I've made the right diagnosis, chosen the proper antibiotics, hired the right candidate for a position. But never in my life have I been more proud of having the answer to a question than in that moment when I told the officer I knew my kidnapper's vehicle registration number.

The information causes a sudden flurry of activity; two policemen move to the corner of the kitchen to use their cell phones. Everyone becomes more animated and more focused, like a group of doctors who have noticed a serious arrhythmia on the cardiac monitor.

Within minutes, it seems, the vehicle has been identified and matched to an individual who is wanted by the police, who has violated parole, and who is suspected of violently assaulting a man in Lubbock.

An officer congratulates me on memorizing the registration number. My dignity is restored, and the strange sense of humiliation that pervaded the room dissipates. I've done at least one thing right. Of course, I would rather have subdued the perpetrator, handcuffed him, and delivered him directly to the police. But for the moment, this feels like the next-best thing.

"Do you know which direction he went?" an officer wants to know.

I tell him with a nod, "Yes, he went down Interstate 40. Headed for New Mexico." I feel like I'm in a cowboy movie: "The gun-man went thadaway, pardner, and as far as I can tell he was hea-din' his horse fer New Mexico."

After about a half hour the chief detective arrives. He's like the department chairman, visiting the wards to see the intriguing case that the residents are all talking about. The fingerprint squad is on its way too. But at the height of the excitement, it's time for me to leave, to go down to the station and make my official state-ment.

Detective Davis drives me downtown. On the way she asks me to identify the ATM we stopped at to see if it has a camera. We drive up and down Bell Street three different times, but I cannot find it. Perhaps I'm more shell-shocked than I realized. Several days later I will easily remember that it was on the corner of Thir-ty-fourth and Bell, and as I thought, it does not have a security camera.

The police station is abandoned when we arrive. Sunday after-noon is not a busy day for crime. Detective Davis has me sit at a cluttered desk and tries to find the official victim's report form on the computer. It takes awhile. She smiles and tells me that she's not used to working without a secretary. If she were a doctor, De-tective Davis would get our top grade for interpersonal skills and for putting the patient at ease. She seems more amused than upset that her Sunday has been interrupted by the first Amarillo kidnapping in years. As she clicks her way through various files, she tells me that most of her experience is in drug-related crime. This is definitely out of the ordinary, for the entire force really.

She finds the form, and I give my story for the third or fourth time in the past hour. In the quiet station, however, I feel that I finally have a chance to relax and really ponder what has just happened to me. I begin to recall details that I haven't reported yet. I tell her how he dug the barrel of the gun into my back while we were in the laundry room. Briefly, we consider whether I should relinquish my T-shirt for gunshot residue, but we both agree that it's probably unnecessary. Interested in every specific, Detective Davis asks me about the firearm.

"Now Dr. Berk, was it a shotgun or a rifle?"

"I don't know. A rifle."

State of Texas v. Jack Lindsey Jordan

> DEFENSE ATTORNEY BAILEY: You made a comment at one point in time that you weren't sure if it was a shotgun or a rifle. Is that correct?
>
> BERK: The first statement says he had a shotgun, okay, and then later on it says I wasn't sure if it was a shotgun or a rifle.
>
> BAILEY: Okay, so today you're stating that you're sure that it was a shotgun? Are you really sure it was a shotgun or could it have been a rifle?
>
> BERK: See, I know more about shotguns and rifles than I did before. It was a shotgun.

As we go over my story, Detective Davis receives a phone call and begins to repeat the whole thing all over again to someone new. I take a moment to gather myself, and without thinking I begin to walk back and forth across the room.

"He's doing really well," says Detective Davis over the phone. "Actually he doesn't seem to be too upset by it," she says as if I'm not there. "Although now he's pacing back and forth," she says, watching me with a smile. I stop and sit back down in the chair.

She eventually hangs up the phone, and we finish filling out the report. I ask her what happens next and she tells me that they will continue the investigation using the information I've given them. They will track down the perpetrator and arrest him. She mentions that the story will run in the newspaper the next day, and I ask her to read it to me. It doesn't mention my name, but describes me as a fifty-five-year-old man. My kidnapper is described as a white male, forty to forty-five years old, five feet eight inches tall, about 175 pounds, with bushy eyebrows. Somehow I smile at the detail.

Detective Davis gives me a ride home, but I immediately go out again to visit my parents' house. I don't want them to hear about the event from someone else, and it's not the type of news that you deliver to your eighty-year-old parents over the phone. I tell them about the kidnapping in broad strokes, leaving out the gunman's threats of revenge. My parents are at a point in their lives when they truly need me, and I want to protect both of them, especially my father, from the more terrifying details of the event. I cannot predict how much publicity my kidnapping will generate in the following weeks and months. For the moment, they are spared the details of the crime.

Finally, I go home to Justin and Shirley. The house has almost returned to normal: the police are gone, and dinner is on the table. The only signs of the day's strange events are the smudges of black powder scattered over various surfaces throughout the house. The fingerprint squad has looked everywhere—door handles, the garage door button, the banister on the stairway—but according to Shirley, they found nothing.

My brother calls me that evening. He's heard the news from

Mom and Dad. I recount the events for the umpteenth time that day and confess how eerie it is to be home now that the police are gone. My brother is concerned about security.

"What do you think the chances are that he would come back?" he asks.

"Oh, I really doubt he would. It just wouldn't be in his best interest. Although he was extremely impulsive. But chances are one in a hundred that he'd come back."

My brother is adamant. "In that case you should have an armed guard."

Earlier that afternoon, the police told us that twenty-four-hour surveillance was not necessary, but later that night I see an Amarillo police car drive slowly down the back alley of our house. I try to sleep that night, but given the extreme emotional stress I've been through, it's difficult. I do the best I can. I'm not sure what the next day has in store, but I suspect that things will be hectic.

Garage door access to our home, which I left open that Sunday morning.

Back alley leading to our garage.

View of Bell Street on a quiet Sunday morning.

The ATM at Thirty-fourth and Bell Street where I tried to make a $500 withdrawal.

Thirty-fourth Street where pavement ends before leaving Amarillo.

Dirt road from Amarillo to Bushland.

Gas station in Bushland where I filled the SUV with gas.

The frontage road leading back to Bushland, which I ran
down once I was released.

11

Jeremy and Justin

The news of my kidnapping spread quickly and generated intense media coverage. Amarillo is a small city, and as the regional dean of the medical school, I was a fairly well-known figure. Though I'd initially hesitated to call the police, I ultimately decided to be open with the public about my experience. In my professional experience, both as a dean and as a physician, I'd found that the best way to deal with a difficult issue is to be forthright and honest. I also thought that my story might have some important public safety lessons, such as always closing your garage door and reacting calmly with dealing with criminal behavior.

When a reporter for the *Amarillo Globe-News* came to my home the day after the kidnapping, I was open to sharing my story with him, as well as with reporters from the three TV news stations who followed. After that, a lot of information became public. The events of my kidnapping were the subject of news reports on television and opinion articles in the local paper. Because I had mentioned my views on gun ownership in one interview, the event got coverage from gun lobbyists at the national level. My story was a vehicle for expressing many different opinions, and it was told from many different perspectives.

However, in all the coverage that my kidnapping generated, there were two versions of the story that never got told. Jeremy remained at school in Massachusetts throughout all of it, and Justin was very private about the entire ordeal, despite how public everything eventually became. I didn't realize at the time how uniquely both boys were affected by what had happened.

Jeremy was two thousand miles away from home on March 6, 2005, but he was the first to suspect that something was wrong that day. Jeremy was a sophomore at Brandeis University, a small, private college in Waltham, Massachusetts. Brandeis is ranked as one of the top thirty-five liberal arts universities in the country, and its students are generally highly motivated, independent, liberal thinking, and accomplished. Though Jeremy has always been extremely bright, personable, and capable, he had not been academically oriented in high school. He was a member of the wrestling team, though, and participated with me in many community activities, even helping me whenever I needed a surrogate patient to demonstrate how to do a physical examination. We had moved from Johnson City to Amarillo at a critical stage of Jeremy's social life, and he had left a lot of close friends behind in Tennessee. Starting over in Texas was difficult, and he did not have the best high school experience. Shirley and I worried that Jeremy's transition to college would be similarly difficult.

However, Jeremy thrived at Brandeis. He dedicated himself to his studies, participated in community activities, and joined one of the few fraternities around campus. We were proud of how well he was managing his time and working out his own priorities. He was earning excellent grades, even in the notoriously difficult Arabic courses that he chose for himself. When it came to writing term papers, Jeremy worked hard and often sought extra help from me. I was always enthusiastic to read his essay drafts and discuss his ideas. He usually had tight deadlines and even had to pull some "all-nighters," so I would always e-mail back my evaluation of content and grammar quickly. Sunday, March 6, was to be a day for such e-mail communication.

His plan that morning was to review my suggestions for his paper and then leave his dorm around eleven so that he could be at the library when it opened. He woke up early, anticipating my e-mail, but by ten thirty it had not arrived. Jeremy began to wonder what was wrong, and expected me to send a message or call at any moment. At the same time that Jeremy was sitting at his computer in his dorm room, waiting for an e-mail from me, I was sitting at my computer in the second-floor study of our house with a gun in my face. Jeremy eventually decided to call the house, but at that point it was empty: Shirley and Justin were at church, and I was driving a stranger's SUV in search of an ATM.

So at about eleven Jeremy called his mom on her cell phone. Shirley told him that I was probably out running, and that I would be back in forty-five minutes. Jeremy was surprised that I had not spoken with him before going out, since I knew he would be waiting for me. Impatient and anxious to get in touch with me, he called the house about half an hour later. Shirley had come home, and I had already come back to the house and left again with her rings.

"Jeremy, you just missed him. He came back to the house and went out again."

"Where's he going?"

"He didn't say. I think he's shopping at a street vendor or something. He took all my rings and my wallet."

Jeremy said that he had never seen a street vendor in Amarillo.

"Well, then maybe there's a garage sale," Shirley suggested.

Certainly garage sales are common on Sunday mornings in Amarillo, although I've never been to one. Jeremy was unconvinced. In the past, when I had arranged to discuss a paper with him, I was always ready and on time. Jeremy ended the call with his mother frustrated and confused.

He spent the rest of the morning irritable, declining his roommates' invitation to go out for coffee, preferring instead to wait in the dorm to hear from me. When the call finally came later that afternoon, it was not what he expected. Shivering from cold and fear, I used a borrowed cell phone from the angelic woman who had stopped her car in Bushland. I was trying to reach Shirley, but dialed Jeremy's number instead.

"I've just been kidnapped. I'll get right back to you."

I delivered the news quickly and did not wait for a response. I don't know how Jeremy reacted, but I can imagine the shock and fear he must have felt on receiving that message. Having waited all day for a word from his father, the first contact we had was a brief, frantic phone call from an unfamiliar number. After worrying for hours, that phone call could only have increased his anxiety. He received another call from his mother just minutes later.

She had spoken to me and was already on her way to Bushland to pick me up. I had not given her much detail about what had happened, and she and Jeremy speculated together that I was probably accosted by a passing car during my run through the neighborhood. Shirley wanted to know what Jeremy thought about her driving the van without carrying a license, which was in the wallet I had taken from her. Shirley has always been very law abiding. Jeremy assured her that it would be all right.

Needless to say, Jeremy spent the rest of the day worrying and had difficulty getting any information, since we were all occupied with police and detectives. Late in the afternoon, I called Justin from the police station and asked him to please e-mail Jeremy the critique I had been writing when the intruder interrupted me. I thought he would appreciate it, but at that point a paper on out-sourcing and the U.S. job economy was not Jeremy's biggest concern. He was worried about my safety, shaken by the thought of me being kidnapped, and above all confused about what had happened and what it meant for us as a family.

Later that evening I called Jeremy and asked him how he was coming on his paper. He said he had not worked on it all day.

"Why not? I sent my comments!"

"Dad, you were kidnapped."

"That's no excuse for being lazy, Jeremy."

It was unfair of me to say, a moment of insensitivity. At that point I didn't realize the effect my kidnapping would have on both me and my family. Perhaps at the time, my perception of what was important was slightly warped. I wanted to trivialize the day's events to minimize their impact on me, but that impulse prevented me from realizing that Jeremy's priorities were the safety of his family. I underestimated how difficult it was for Jeremy to be so far away from family during a crisis. For us at home, the stress of the ordeal was immediate and intense, but for Jeremy the event was no less disruptive.

Jeremy has always been very family oriented. Though he

showed a great deal of independence when he moved away for college, he still stayed strongly connected with everything that was going on at home. He would call home every day, whether it was to talk to me and Shirley, tease Justin, or update his grandparents about what he was doing in school; he enjoyed having long conversations with the people he loved. Being so out of the loop during the events of March 6 would have made him feel incredibly frustrated and lonely.

I imagine that throughout the chaos of the kidnapping and its aftermath, Jeremy wanted very much to come home. He understood how serious and dangerous the situation was, and I'm sure he realized how close he came to losing his father forever. It was a unique challenge to deal with those intense thoughts and emotions so far from home. But Jeremy was incredibly resilient. He stayed at school and continued to devote himself admirably to his studies, to participate normally in college life, and to support and cherish his family as he had always done.

March 6 started out as a typical Sunday for Justin as well. He was in the downstairs game room playing his guitar and waiting to be picked up by his friend Brandon. They had developed a routine of attending services at the Southwest Church of Christ together, and Brandon was going to pick Justin up at nine thirty. The boys were looking forward to a church-sponsored missionary trip to Brazil that summer. I had encouraged the endeavor, since I understood Justin's impulse to serve. While I tried not to influence his long-term career decisions, it was always obvious to me that Justin would make an outstanding physician. I would never discourage him from pursuing the missionary path that I once hoped to follow.

Just a little after nine thirty, Justin came upstairs to meet Brandon at the front door. I stuck my head out of the laundry room and said good-bye, and he left the house without incident. The next he heard from me, I was calling from his mother's phone, telling him that it was dangerous to go home, that he should spend the day with Brandon. As with Jeremy, I didn't give him very much information, and the phone call must have been just as scary and confusing. How strange it must have been for Justin to try to interact normally with his friend after getting the message that his father had been kidnapped. It must have been stranger still to be called home to a house full of police officers who wanted to talk to him and confirm my story.

When he walked through the front door, we gave each other the biggest hug of my life. It was the most emotional moment of my day, and the only time that I shed tears related to the event. For me, they expressed an overwhelming happiness for what had not occurred, an intense feeling of relief and gratitude that we were both alive. I think Justin had a mature sense of the dangerous nature of what had happened, and both of us were glad just to see each other again.

That evening, Justin was interviewed by two officers who asked him to confirm my story. It was at that point that Justin must have realized that he was in the house at the same time as the gunman, that he had even talked to me while the stranger pointed a gun at my back. No doubt it was a terrifying realization. In recalling the events of the day for the police, Justin said he remembered some apprehension in my voice when he left the house. Later, he wondered if maybe he had seen strange shadows in the laundry room behind me, but I don't think that was possible from the angle where he stood. However, whether or not he had any suspicions or fears at that moment, I can understand why his memory of it would come with an intense mix of emotions. Perhaps he wishes that he had noticed something that day, that he had done something different, but there was no way he could have known I was in danger.

I also look back on that moment of Justin leaving the house and remember the anguish surrounding it. There were so many things I wanted to tell him as he walked out the door. I knew at that point that I might not survive the day, and yet I couldn't tell him good-bye. I didn't have the opportunity to at least choose my parting words to him, leave some instructions for the rest of his life. I was not given that chance. The gunman had taken that from me. I was like a man in the final seconds of a sudden heart attack, or a victim gasping for his dying breath in the aftermath of a car accident: I could see death, but I could not say good-bye to the people I loved most. I could not say a word to my son standing right in front of me.

If I had been given the chance to speak to him as he walked out our front door, I would have told Justin, first, that if things went wrong he should not look back. *Justin, this event reflects nothing on us. It was a mouse, an open garage door, our proximity to I-27. It is not our fault. You could not have suspected what was happening.* Then I would have told him:

I want to be around to advise you, to guide you as you learn how to use your enormous talents. I have not wanted to push you into medicine, though I know you would be a fine physician. You have the compassion, the aequanimitas, and the fantastic mind. There is no better way to make contributions than to combine your compassion with scientific knowledge that can heal, cure, enlighten. Physicians go where even the finest pastors cannot go, and you would make an ideal addition to the profession. But if you choose medicine, Justin, never make it a business. If you're making $500,000 a year and refusing to see Medicaid patients, it is time to get out of the field. Whatever you choose to do, make sure you are giving back to the community that has supported you. There is great honor in being a math professor, a researcher, a musician, as long as you are part of your community and find a way to make life better for others.

If you choose medicine, there will be hundreds around the country eager to assist you. It is part of the Hippocratic Oath—to teach the sons and daughters of those who have taught you the art of medicine. They will be everywhere, not just Boston, Johnson City, and Amarillo, but Dallas, San Antonio, Nashville, Memphis.

I see someone taking you to the bedside of a patient with liver disease. Now Justin, this is what your dad taught me many years ago. Look at the sclera, the white of the eye. Assess the color, and you can determine the level of liver damage that way. Always look at the sclera and skin in room light, be sure the room itself has not been painted yellow. It takes practice, but eventually you will be able to correlate skin and sceral color with the measurement of bilirubin in the blood. Look for the small abnormalities in the skin called spider angiomata that also indicate liver disease. They occur because the liver is failing to break down estrogen and estrogen is stimulating the growth of these lesions. In the same way, you can find redness over the palm of the hand, more on the side of the thumb. It is called palmar erythema. You can determine the size of the liver by percussion: the liver has a flatter sound than the lung or bowel, so you can determine its size like a carpenter determines where the studs are behind a wall. Put your hand here, just below the rib cage. Ask the patient to take a deep breath, and you will feel the edge of the liver meet your fingertips. You can always tell whether or not there is any fluid or ascites in the abdomen. *Your dad always said that an ultrasound was unnecessary. He was never wrong about the presence or absence of ascites on exam. Have the patient stretch his hands outward as if stopping traffic. Lightly put pressure with your fingers against his—a fine flapping of his finger against yours confirms the liver is failing and that coma may soon follow.*

But most of all, Justin, listen to what the patient has to say. That will be your best clue to what to do. Your dad told us so many stories to make this point. Like the time he saw a patient with pneumonia with no obvious cause who was getting worse each day. Finally, the patient told him about the sick parakeet that he had taken care of. The parakeet died, but he bought another and put it in the same cage. It died too, and another after that. That information made the diagnosis: parakeet pneumonia, or psittacosis. The key to the diagnosis was with the patient all along. Or the young woman who had given birth at the City Hospital and then started spiking high fevers of 104. It was a mystery, since there had been no complications and no infection related to delivery. But then she told your dad about her trip to rural Africa, where she saw so many people with malaria who were sick just like she was. Whether it leads to a diagnosis or not, listening to your patient is the touchstone to success.

These were the things I wanted to tell Justin as he walked out the door and I contemplated saying good-bye to him forever. I will always be grateful that I was given another chance to tell him these things. Immediately following my kidnapping, I wanted to make the event seem less important than it actually was. I did not want it to interfere with Jeremy's work at school. I did not want to think about how things might have ended differently and changed the lives of my family forever. But the truth is that the events of March 6 did change things for all of us. Above all, it showed me clearly how important it is to be thankful for family. I should never pass up an opportunity to tell my sons how proud they make me and how much they mean to me.

Fortunately, my anguished good-bye from the laundry room was not the last word I spoke to Justin. An incomplete collection of thoughts about outsourcing was not my last message to Jeremy. I survived to tell both boys how much I love them. I lived to advise Justin about his future, and I lived to see Jeremy graduate from college with honors.

12

A New Day

I awoke on March 7 with the sun brightly shining through my window. I had no intention of reporting to work. Physician and regional dean, I was about to become better known as the kidnapped doctor who left his garage door open. I would also become a Panhandle gunslinger.

At about ten o'clock, an Amarillo detective, Sergeant James, came to my house with a photo lineup for me to look at. He had a printed sheet with a group of six pictures on it. They were all driver's license photos of middle-aged white males. Before showing me the sheet, Sergeant James warned me that this type of lineup could be very tricky, that the pictures might be old, and that the individuals might be smiling unlike they would be while committing a crime.

"It can be hard to recognize someone in a photo lineup, so take your time."

I looked at the photos and recognized the kidnapper immediately. I pointed to him without a moment's hesitation.

"That's him. I will never, never forget what he looked like."

"How certain are you?" Sergeant James asked me.

"Certain. I am 100 percent certain that this is the man."

State of Texas v. Jack Lindsey Jordan

DISTRICT ATTORNEY BLOUNT: I'll show you what has been marked as state exhibit 16 and I'll ask you if you recognize that.

SERGEANT DAVID JAMES: Yes sir, I do. It is a photo lineup.

BLOUNT: Now is this the lineup you showed to Dr. Berk?

JAMES: Yes sir, it is.

BLOUNT: By the time you showed this lineup to Dr. Berk, you had developed a suspect in the kidnapping case?

JAMES: Yes sir.

BLOUNT: And did you include a photo of that suspect as one of the six photos in that array?

JAMES: Yes sir.

BLOUNT: And when you showed it to him, did you tell him beforehand that there was one particular guy in there who you thought had done it?

JAMES: No sir.

BLOUNT: Did Dr. Berk review the photo lineup?

JAMES: Yes, he did. He glanced at all of them and identified photograph number 5.

BLOUNT: Okay, what was his reaction?

JAMES: I can't say what his reaction was, but there was no doubt in his mind who had done this to him.

BLOUNT: Did you ask him to do anything in regards to the lineup?

JAMES: Yes, I had him initial next to that photo.

> BLOUNT: And Sergeant, the photo that Dr. Berk picked out is
> a photograph of Jack Lindsey Jordan?
>
> JAMES: Yes sir, and in the details of the photo lineup, in [Dr.
> Berk's] handwriting, it says "positively" and under that it
> says "100%."

Sergeant James told me that I had identified a man named Jack
Lindsey Jordan.

"He's a dangerous and violent criminal. He beat up a guy in
Lubbock the day before your kidnapping, gave him twenty stitches in the face. You're lucky he didn't harm you."

I was elated. My abductor had a name. Jack Lindsey Jordan. An
all-points bulletin was issued for his arrest; he was wanted for
aggravated kidnapping. I hoped very much that the search would
lead to his capture. Though I felt safe enough to joke about the
kidnapper with close friends, I had taken his threats extremely
seriously. In fact, the day before, I had asked Sergeant James
whether perhaps I should get a gun to protect myself and my
family in case the kidnapper returned. He assured me that criminals rarely return to the scene of a crime, and that the gunman
probably could not find my house if he wanted to. He also pointed out that owning a gun without having the proper training
might be more of a liability than a safeguard. When I pressed the
issue, Sergeant James urged me to wait a week and then look into
taking a class if I was still interested.

Despite his reassurances, however, I was still deeply worried
that Jordan would realize that I had contacted the police, that he
would come back to carry out his threats. In the quiet moments
of my morning, I experienced vivid daydreams.

*The gunman breaks into my house wielding the same shotgun he
had the day before. He is angry and hostile.*

"Berk, you know you shouldn't have gotten the police involved in this. I let you go because I thought you understood me. But now I'm facing kidnapping . . . that's the worst charge I've ever had, Berk. What were you thinking? You know how angry I can get, and now you've pushed me too far."

I remembered Jordan's moment of intense rage when I could not find the garage door opener the day before. I envisioned the shotgun (yes, now I knew the difference between a shotgun and a rifle) and once again pictured the gaping wound it could leave in my head or chest. I thought about how helpless I had felt with that gun pointed at my back, and I imagined how different things would have been if I had had a gun myself. *Yes,* I thought, *the only difference between the two of us was that he had a gun.*

That afternoon, I talked to my wife about purchasing a firearm.

"Shirley, I've thought about it. I really do want to get a gun. Today. No waiting a week."

Shirley had been a gun owner her entire life. She had always seen the value of owning a personal firearm, and the events of the day before had done nothing to change that. She told me we could go buy a gun together, and she drove me to the nearest gun dealer we could find.

We pulled into the tiny parking lot of Panhandle Gunslingers, "Amarillo's Place to Shoot." It was in the middle of downtown Amarillo, a small, dark, squat rectangular building on the corner of Georgia and Eighth Avenue. There was a small shooting range located just to the right of the entrance, and when we walked into the shop that day, we saw a small, middle-aged woman using the range for target practice. Just as we entered, the woman's gun jammed, so Shirley and I took a look around the store while the owner helped her with the firearm.

There were only a few handguns on display, but ironically they had an enormous number of hunting rifles. After browsing their selection, we decided to buy a gun in Shirley's name. I had given my wallet to the detectives for fingerprinting, so I had no cash, and Jordan had kept my credit cards when he left me behind in Bushland.

Shirley and I approached one of the clerks behind the counter. He was a soft-spoken, middle-aged man who was courteous and did not ask a lot of questions. He told us we could buy a gun, get it registered, and conduct an identity check, all in a matter of minutes. I pointed to a gun in the display case that looked appealing. He took it out and told me that it was a revolver, a Ruger GP100.

"It has six chambers for .38-caliber bullets," he explained.

The name and the description didn't mean very much to me, but I liked the way it felt in my hand, cold and heavy. I admired its gleaming silver body and the wood-grain handle lined with hard black rubber. It looked like a nice gun for a gentleman.

"It costs $400, but ammunition comes cheap," said the salesman behind the counter. "You get one lesson included free of charge."

We made the purchase using Shirley's credit card and went home. I felt better knowing that if Jack Lindsey Jordan decided to come back, I would no longer be helpless to defend my home and family. I was extremely happy with my decision.

Later that afternoon, a reporter for the *Amarillo Globe-News* came to the house to talk to me. He was a friend of mine, someone who had covered stories about the medical school many times since I had become dean. I knew he was always accurate and professional, and I felt comfortable talking to him.

The reporter asked me about the details of my kidnapping,

and he was particularly interested in how I had managed to stay calm though it all. I answered his questions just as I had those of the police officers the night before. At the end of the interview, he asked me if I had any initial reactions to the event and what had happened to me. I told him frankly that it made me want to own a gun.

I was quoted in the article: "The one thing I want to do today is get a gun. Not so much for a future robbery of my house but for this particular individual if he were to come back here. Because the interesting thing you think about was the difference between him and me . . . he's got a gun and I don't."[3]

On Tuesday evening, Sergeant James called me with an air of concern in his voice. "Jack Jordan may have come back to Amarillo!"

13

Crime, Drugs, and Guns

I had always supported gun control, and I never thought I would one day become a gun owner. But the kidnapping changed my opinion about this issue. Indeed, the kidnapping made me think very carefully about several subjects that I had not spent much time thinking about before. For three days following the abduction, I did not go into work, but spent time at home, thinking and writing about the topics of gun ownership, drug use, and crime. Of course, I already held certain views about these subjects, but now I was considering them from a much more personal perspective. I was no longer just a father, a physician, the dean of a medical school. I was also a crime victim: the kidnapped doctor. In the days following March 6, reevaluating my views on crime, drugs, and guns was an important part of contextualizing and coming to terms with what had happened to me.

Crime in Texas

State of Texas v. Jack Lindsey Jordan

DISTRICT ATTORNEY BLOUNT, Closing Argument:
I'm tired of feeling as though I don't have the right to leave
my garage door open. I bet Dr. Berk is tired of people saying,
"You know that was kind of stupid." Why shouldn't he be
allowed to leave it open? Why can't I? Why can't you? Why
have we got to the point where we just accept it's a fact of
life that we are going to be victims? I'm tired of it and you
should be too.

In the days following my kidnapping, I thought about who was
responsible for what had happened. I foolishly left my garage
door open and the inside door unlocked. Jack Lindsey Jordan entered my house with a shotgun intent to steal cash. He was a repeat offender, a career criminal. When he was released on parole
in 2004, he could have looked for a job and returned to life as a
normal citizen. Instead he reestablished his habits of drug abuse
and crime. Perhaps his time in prison did not give him the resources needed to adjust to a lawful life. Although I don't blame
the Texas Department of Criminal Justice for the crime that Jack
Lindsey Jordan committed, I do strongly believe that certain
things could have been done to make his crime—and all crimes
committed by repeat offenders—less likely.

It is not surprising that incarceration does not end the cycle of
crime. These individuals leave prison more hardened to life's re-
alities, more enmeshed in a network of criminal behavior, more
likely to blame society for their plight, more drug-addicted, phys-

ically stronger, and more rejected by society than ever. I was kidnapped by a criminal who was probably more dangerous after being released from prison than when he first went in.

The prison system in Texas does attempt to reform its inmates. Yet, about half of all inmates released from Texas prisons come back within three years. The Texas Department of Criminal Justice has resource centers that are supposed to provide prisoners with the opportunity to seek family and marriage counseling, job skills counseling, spiritual counseling, and life skills training. However, most of these centers are underfunded. Perhaps there is an underlying feeling that truly violent criminals are incapable of reform, that all prisoners are remorseless sociopaths who would not benefit from psychological counseling. Whatever the reason for the lack of resources, most prisoners never receive the counseling or training that they need during their incarcerations.[4]

While prison work programs also exist, attempts at preparing inmates to enter the labor force after their release are similarly ineffective. Texas law requires prisoners to work if they are physically able, but the work status of inmates is not followed carefully and probably less than half actually perform prison jobs. Moreover, the jobs a prisoner can perform require very few marketable skills, providing only marginal opportunities for employment on the outside. Ultimately, prison industry programs are designed to bring in revenue, not to provide vocational training for its workers.[5]

Prisons try to provide drug counseling, as drugs and crime go hand in hand. Beyond the dangerous and violent culture that immediately surrounds the sale and purchase of illegal drugs, drug addiction itself breeds violence and crime.

Thomas Jefferson said that the first duty of government was to protect its people. Had the State of Texas done its job in protecting me from Jack Jordan? Are repeat offenders career criminals who have chosen a life of crime? Are they sociopaths and psychopaths who have no conscience? Are they individuals who are hopeless threats to society, preying on the weak and naive?

Or are there those who cry out for help as Jordan seemed to be doing for a moment? Are there repeat offenders who have been shortchanged in life, handicapped by childhood abuse or poverty, addicted to drugs so they become in need of medical help, their brains forever scarred by toxic drug effects? Surely, there are those who can turn their lives around with the right opportunity, reconnect with God, family, or society.

On our ride to Bushland, I told Jordan "Man, you need help."

He replied, "Who is going to help me, Berk? You?"

Was this man a sociopathic killer or a man who had made too many mistakes? Of those mistakes, few could be worse than methamphetamine addiction.

Methamphetamine—Mother of All Mistakes

Physicians have long accepted that alcohol and drug addiction are a disease. Drugs affect both mind and body in specific ways. Often when we are searching for the answers to aberrant or criminal behavior among human beings, the answer lies in mood-altering, behavior-altering drugs.

Unfortunately, we in the medical profession often must treat our own addicted colleagues. Physicians and nurses around the country steal drugs every day and use drugs even when caring for patients. Anesthesiologists in training are the worst offenders. For whatever reason—access to mood-altering drugs, stress on the job, lack of control in the operating room, or observation of the positive aspects of drugs seen in patients—these doctors often become addicted to drugs and use their job to gain access to whatever drugs they are using. The nursing field is plagued by good nurses who use their respect on the job to steal and use pain medications, narcotics, or anti-anxiety drugs.

Physicians know when to suspect drug addiction in their own. Doctors who once were totally competent and reliable have a change in behavior. Perhaps they start coming to work late, start making costly mistakes, develop problems at home, or change jobs and locations. Almost all physicians have had experience with drug-addicted colleagues. When a physician or nurse is suspected of being addicted, he or she is confronted by a supervisor, administrator, or colleague. If he admits to the problem, he goes for rehabilitation—rehabilitation, not prison. For months, or longer, he may receive treatment, usually away from his home in a unit where he is cut off from the outside world until he is better. If rehab is successful, he will get back his license to practice medicine, with some sponsor observing the success of his rehabilitation. He may go to a new place to start over, but his career continues. He has been rehabilitated.

Jordan was hooked on methamphetamines. I say that because he directly told me so, and I cannot see why he would lie to me about that. Surely he had nothing to gain. When he entered my home he told me that he was running from the law, but he later said that he was in need of drugs and in need of help. He spoke specifically of meth and its expense.

Methamphetamine abuse is on the rise around the country. It is a very powerful stimulant drug. It may be smoked, snorted, swallowed, or injected. It causes a rush or high that can last half a day. The high is caused by the release of a hormone in the brain called dopamine, a chemical that regulates feelings of pleasure.[6]

Jordan was not high on methamphetamine when he kidnapped me. I would have recognized that behavior. It is likely, however, that he was experiencing the long-term effects of such abuse.

Methamphetamine violence has gone out of control. The production, distribution, and abuse of methamphetamines are, more than with any other drug, likely to be associated with violent crime. In addition, violent crimes are committed to obtain money to purchase these drugs every day, in all states of the United States.[7]

The Methamphetamine Treatment Project studied the psychological effects of the drug on more than one thousand users in several different states. Twenty-seven percent of the study participants had tried to commit suicide. Forty-three percent of them had been involved in some type of violent behavior and reported that they had trouble controlling violent behavior.[8] Imagine an addictive drug pervasive in our society that causes almost half the users to have violent behavior that they cannot control. Most of these episodes of violent behavior, especially in those who injected the drug, involved assaults and assault weapons. The report warns physicians that caring for these patients will be associated with high levels of violence and anger management problems. Interpersonal violence can be expected as part of these individuals' everyday existence.[9]

To the lay public, what does this mean? Methamphetamine abuse is on the increase in the United States, and people addicted to these drugs are very, very dangerous. In fact, they are brain damaged, and the damage itself likely encourages violent behavior and anger. In the United States today, many homicides, armed robberies, assaults, and perhaps kidnappings are the result of methamphetamine-addicted people. There are so many Jack Lindsey Jordans who remain in society, and there are so many garage doors that remain open. Were Jordan to come to our clinic with complaints of anxiety, depression, or an infection where he had injected drugs, we would treat him, advocate for him, advise him, and try to protect him from himself.

I continue to believe in the model of drug addiction as a disease. I have had patients addicted to drugs for whom I advocated and did not judge them. Fortunately, I usually did not know the extent of their criminal behavior. Many HIV-positive patients got their disease from illegal intravenous drug abuse. They were treated no differently from those who got the disease by a blood transfusion. I have also helped too many health-care professionals through alcohol or narcotics addiction, believing them to be good people despite the history of terrible lapses in their professional responsibility.

I cannot excuse or defend Jordan's behavior—his uncontrolled anger directed at me, his threats, his lies, his crimes of kidnapping and robbery. But I can try to understand it from the perspective of a human being. From this perspective I can view the situation with hope. If drug addiction is a disease, then perhaps it has a cure. If a criminal shows remorse, then perhaps he is capable of true penance and reform. Before my kidnapping, I never thought much about how society should respond to drugs and crime. Now I have a stake in a prison system that needs to be dedicated to the goals of reform and rehabilitation.

The Right to Bear Arms and Other Rights

My dad woke me early in the morning on June 6, 1968, to tell me that Bobby Kennedy had been assassinated. I was devastated. He was a hero, an individual who had given many college students of the time a hope for a better day. Now he was the victim of a lunatic with a handgun. So when the Gun Control Act of 1968 was passed, I was an advocate, as was everyone I knew. Restrictions on gun ownership seemed a small price to pay to keep innocent people from being killed.

Later, as a physician, I saw the terrible risk of guns in the accidents they caused and the suicides that they facilitated. I remember such terrible stories as the man who came home at night to the sounds of somebody in his closet. He got his gun, opened the closet door, confirmed someone was in there, and shot to death his young daughter, who was hiding from him as a prank. What could be worth this type of tragedy? And every physician knows of teenagers who while at home alone decided to commit suicide using the family gun.

There is a cliché, however, that a conservative is a mugged liberal. I believe that now. One of the first observations that I made after my kidnapping was that the intruder had a gun and I did not. Two middle-aged men, the same size; one had a gun and one did not. He took me from my home and had me do what he wanted. There was no help from police or anyone else. I was on my own. Should there be another such crime in my home, I want to have the possibility of protection. In the days following the kidnapping, I did not feel protected. He had made a very specific and forceful threat against my family, and even though I was a well-known person in the Amarillo community, still I was totally vulnerable to this person should he have decided to return in a rage.

Someone told me recently that she had been taught never to leave home and get into a car at gunpoint under any circumstances. I don't know if that is advice normally given or not. However, if the choice was between having a chance to use a gun against an intruder and getting into someone's car, I would prefer the gun the next time. I don't want to press my luck.

I once found it amusing that someone would want a machine gun or other rapid-fire weapon to defend their home. Now, I'm no longer amused. Whatever makes them comfortable, they should have that right—coupled with the knowledge and responsibility of gun safety. I know that not everyone will understand this concept—that it is very important to be able to protect oneself from a bully with a gun. Differences in viewpoint are of course determined by different life experiences.

Coincidently, only a few weeks after my kidnapping I had the opportunity to host Senator John Cornyn, U.S. senator from Texas, when he visited the Texas Tech School of Medicine in Amarillo. Senator Cornyn was instrumental in establishing a strong set of victim's rights for crime victims in Texas when he served as attorney general of the state. These rights include:

The right to protection from harm and threats of harm arising from cooperation with prosecution efforts.

The right to have your safety and that of your family taken into consideration when bail is being considered.

The right to be informed about court proceedings, including cancellations and rescheduling.

The right to information about procedures in criminal investigations and in the criminal justice system.

The right to receive information about the Texas crime victims' compensation fund and referral to social service agencies.

The right to provide information to a probation department about the impact of the offense upon you and your family.

The right to be notified about parole proceedings, to participate in the parole process, and to be notified of the in-
mate's release.

The right to be present at all public court proceedings related
to the offense if the presiding judge approves.

The right to a safe waiting area before and during court proceedings.

The right to prompt return of any property that is no longer
needed as evidence.

The right to have the prosecutor notify your employer that the
need for your testimony may involve your absence from
work.

The right to counseling, on request, regarding AIDS and HIV
infection if the offense is a sexual assault.[10]

I hope all states will adopt similar rights for victims of crime.

Texas now gives crime victims an even greater right. Spon-
sored by Senator Wentworth of San Antonio, a Texas Tech School
of Law graduate, a bill passed called the Castle Doctrine gives
Texans the right to attack an intruder in their home, car, or work-
place. In Austin, Texas, in 2008, Senator Wentworth stated: "People don't have to wonder if the person in front of them is armed
or whether the gun is loaded. If they feel threatened they have the
right to defend themselves, without having to worry about being
charged with a crime or being sued."[11]

I have a great love for Amarillo, Lubbock, and the State of Texas. I want to be able to own a gun, carry a concealed weapon, and
have the protections of a crime victim that this state has provided

me. And yes, I appreciate having the clearly delineated right to shoot the next intruder who might enter my home.

Once a criminal comes into your home and is a potential threat to members of your family, you will never, ever feel the same about this issue. Those who have had similar experiences to mine will want the right to own a gun.

The Right Prescription

14

On Tuesday evening, a call from Sergeant James was momentarily frightening. "Jordan appears to have returned to Amarillo and bought a gun at Panhandle Gunslingers," he told me. I went from frightened to embarrassed. Panhandle Gunslingers is where I bought my gun. An easy resolution. Jordan was being tracked with the use of my stolen credit card. Shirley had a duplicate of the credit card, and we were foolish enough to use it to pay for our gun. The gun was our purchase, not Jordan's.

In the days after the crime, I was not the only one thinking over the event and what it meant. For several days the story was in bold headlines on the front page of the *Amarillo Globe-News,* the city's only newspaper: "After Beating Odds, Texas Dean Relives Ordeal." It was the article for which I had been interviewed on the day after the kidnapping.

Suspect Sought After Berk Survives Kidnapping Nightmare

It took Steven Berk two hours to survive the often un-survivable. Berk, the regional dean of Texas Tech University Health Sciences Center in Amarillo was kidnapped at gunpoint at 9:15 a.m. Sunday from his Puckett neighborhood home.

He spent the next two hours riding around Potter and Randall counties with an angry and agitated criminal.

Berk, also an internal medicine specialist, said his medical experience kept him calm and in control. It also might have saved him from a far worse fate.

"Being calm is what we do," Berk said, adding there was no advantage to getting panicky.

Otherwise, the story might have ended differently.

As it was, Berk made it home safely and, late Monday, Amarillo police secured a Randall County warrant for the arrest of Jack Lindsey Jordan, 41. The warrant was for aggravated kidnapping in connection with the episode. Jordan also has a [sic] outstanding warrant for a parole violation from Texas State Pardons and Paroles, according to a news release from the Amarillo Police Department.[12]

The article went on to describe the visits to the gas stations and ATM machines, the return home, and the trip to Bushland. It included my statements about wanting a gun, and then quoted an Amarillo officer who offered an explanation for why the crime had occurred.

The house was probably chosen because the garage door was left up. . . . The garage door was unsecured, and that's why that place was chosen. As usual, it was a crime of opportunity.[13]

The article highlighted the value of staying calm during a dangerous confrontation, as well as the incredible importance of doing small things to secure your home against criminals, like closing your garage door. People responded to these lessons positively, and I felt that my story was being used, in some small way, as a public service. The response to my comments about gun ownership was also very positive. Over the next few days I received dozens of e-mails and phone calls from people who wanted to offer me shooting lessons or help me purchase a gun. Several told me about how they had shot criminals in or just outside of their homes, or how they had been robbed at home or at gunpoint on the street. We commiserated as crime victims and as gun owners, and I appreciated the outpouring of support from friends, acquaintances, and strangers alike. I was surprised by how much commentary my experience was generating; it seemed like everyone had something to say.

Just a few days after the first article, an editorial appeared in the *Globe* entitled "Doctor Has Right Prescription for Life-and-Death Situation." The writer commended me for having the presence of mind to memorize Jordan's vehicle registration number and considered my actions a good lesson about dealing with crime. But while some people described my exploits as a kidnapping victim in a positive way, others argued that I had done some things wrong. A few were particularly critical of the fact that I "allowed" the kidnapper to return to my home. Some told me that getting into the car with the gunman was the first worst mistake I could have made. Others continued to point out the many opportunities I had to escape. In the end, however, my experience was considered a success. No one could deny that I made it through unharmed, that I kept my family out of danger, and that I retained a vital piece of information that led to the identification of Jack Jordan as the perpetrator of the crime. Following my kidnapping, the messages of support and approval far outweighed the criticisms.

Beyond being taken as a practical lesson, my experience touched an emotional chord in the community. There may have been several reasons for this. First, I shared my experience openly with everyone, agreeing to tell the whole story honestly and completely to the newspaper and radio and TV stations. My detectives did not recommend this, but, as they said, the choice was mine. I thought it was important to have the incident discussed, especially since Amarillo is considered a very low crime area and there were many people here who always kept their garage doors open. One TV station did a story specifically designed as a public service announcement. They even videotaped my open garage door and traced the route of the intruder into my house as a warning to always keep your doors locked. Second, although Amarillo was the only place I called home, many people realized that I was not originally from West Texas. They regretted that I had become the victim of a West Texas crime, and they made an effort to show me how welcome and safe I should feel in my adopted community.

I was appreciative of the many letters and e-mails expressing concern and respect for me, not only from friends in Amarillo but also from old friends and colleagues all over the country, particularly from East Tennessee.

> I was so sorry to hear of your recent traumatic event
> with the armed intruder in your home. I know it is at times
> like these that we begin thinking and contemplating very

quickly about our priorities here on earth. Obviously, God had other plans for you. I pray that through this emotional and devastating experience you would be open to hear his voice speak clearly to you: to whom much is given much is required. I am thankful that your life was spared.

I can't imagine how scary that must have been to have someone come into your home with a gun. I am so glad that you were calm and are safe and well. You are such a kind man. I'm sure that came through to save you. You are in our thoughts and prayers.

I was mortified when I turned on the news last night and saw you and heard the story. I am so glad you came through the ordeal physically unscathed. Your demeanor may very well have saved your life. Thanks for so openly sharing your experience.

I wanted you to know how proud of you I am. You are truly a hero; you saved yourself and your family. Thank you for the calm spirit you have. The respect and support you have received through this is, I am sure, overwhelming.

You are in our minds and hearts. It is a shame that it takes such an extraordinary event to express concern and gratitude but I just can't imagine this place without you and your incredible dedication to all of us in this community. I'm thanking God that you, Shirley and Justin are safe.

Wow, what an adventure and my deepest respect for keeping your cool. Our thoughts and prayers are with you.

We are proud to read your story. It confirms the good things we knew about you already. Sorry it had to be demonstrated so stressfully to you and yours. We have lots of experience with firearms—let us know if we can help.

I can't tell you how glad I am that you were able to survive your ordeal. As a trauma survivor, I know what kind of impact something like that can have. It is a shame that we live in a world where wonderful people like Steve Berk have to face that kind of trouble. Thank goodness you kept your head but then again you always had such a calming personality.

Just thought you could use a smile. Our church prayed for you today. Heroic acts come in all shapes and sizes. I would put yours above any. Your family came first, at all cost, with no exceptions. You are without a doubt a hero in our eyes. We are proud of you, proud to know you, proud to work for you. Thanks for the privilege of working for you.

I know God is with you and your family. Watching over you day and night. I read Psalm 23 this morning and thought of you. It took on a whole new meaning. May God hold you in the palm of his hand.

While friends, colleagues, and even strangers reached out to me after the kidnapping, another major response to the event was pure curiosity. Crime was not an everyday event in Amarillo, and the public wanted to learn every detail about what happened and who was involved. Once Jack Lindsey Jordan's name was released, stories began to appear about him, both in Amarillo and elsewhere. There were reports about other victims he had terrorized in the days leading up to my kidnapping: a Lubbock man whose injuries had put him in the hospital and a woman from Meadow who had been robbed at gunpoint in her own home. Newspaper reporters and TV stations in Texas and New Mexico were especially eager to find out about Jordan's past, and stories about his earlier crimes and his wife's suspicious death surfaced. The *Amarillo Globe-News* ran a story describing Jordan as a "psycho," based on an interview with his deceased wife's sister. It began: "Angry, impulsive, violent. That is how Dana Carmon remembers her brother-in-law, Jack Lindsey Jordan, 41." In the article, Carmon went on to describe Jordan as abusive and dangerous, and she blamed Jordan for her sister's death.[14] Trying to get every angle on the story, reporters also found Linda Hamilton, Jordan's sister, who lived in Sugar Land, Texas. She told the *Lubbock Avalanche-Journal* that before this most recent crime spree, her brother had been living with their parents. "He seemed to be OK," she told the newspaper. "When all of this came about, I was just very floored. He talked about how desperately he hated prison. Why did he risk going back?"[15] Hamilton was quoted as saying: "Things have been pretty much a struggle for my brother in the past. . . . He never wanted to accept responsibility for his own actions. I think years back if he had gotten some type of psychological help, he would have been OK."[16]

In the days following the kidnapping, I watched the news reports and read the articles like everyone else. The different accounts and opinions about Jack Jordan made me want to understand more about the violent, enigmatic person whose frustrating life had intersected with mine.

15

Jack Lindsey Jordan

J ack Lindsey Jordan grew up in Seminole, Texas, a small community located in Gaines County. Seminole is and always has been a conservative community with traditional values. Its economy has depended on Texas oil fields since the 1920s. Jack was the son of a successful businessman—a homebuilder and furniture store owner. His mother was well liked in the community. His grandfather was part of the Hoffman Oil Company. After my kidnapping, several acquaintances in West Texas who had known Jack or his family volunteered stories of how they remembered him. As a child, Jack was not wanting for things, as his family was among the wealthiest in Seminole. Although his dad left the family when Jack was still young, he was not abused or otherwise mistreated. His mother remarried several times, but for the most part Jack led a fairly typical childhood. Nothing stands out as a potential cause or predictor for the criminal path his life would eventually take.

Jack was mischievous at a young age, but not mean. When he was eight years old, he somehow obtained a set of firecrackers. As he was setting them off, one went off in his hands, causing a great deal of pain and minor burns. That evening he nursed his injuries and lamented that he had not finished lighting the entire package. The next day he was at it again, popping firecrackers for an amused audience of older kids. Again a firecracker went off prematurely, in his same injured hand.

Jack was also known for his bike riding, and he got a lot of attention from other children with his daredevil tricks, popping wheelies and making risky jumps on homemade ramps. He was a loner but always wanting to impress.

As a teenager, Jack moved from Seminole to Hobbs, New Mexico, where he attended Hobbs High School. He drove cars too fast, and he probably used and perhaps sold marijuana. But for the most part, Jack stayed out of trouble, and he was never convicted of any crimes as a minor. After high school, Jack moved to Memphis, Tennessee, and got a job as a construction worker. In 1986, when he was twenty-four, Jack met a woman named Lisa and married her. According to Dana Carmon, Lisa Jordan's sister, that was about the time that Jack started showing aggressive and violent tendencies. Carmon remembers several instances that made her worry that Jack was not a good match for her sister.

One weekend he asked to play golf with Dana's husband and another two friends. The group was taken aback when Jack, far from the clubhouse, decided to urinate on the green in between putts. Jack was nonchalant. He did not judge others and did not care to be judged by them. Dana's husband returned home to announce that this man was not your average golf partner.

Once a car cut Jack off in the midst of traffic. At a traffic light

Jack got out of the car, put his hands through the driver's-side window, and began to beat up the driver who had cut him off. His temper was fierce.

According to Dana, Jack very much wanted Lisa to become pregnant, but as soon as she gave birth to Austin Lindsey Jordan in 1989, his behavior became worse. He began drinking heavily and would often go out of town to find work. When Dana called the house to speak with Lisa, Jack would tell her to stay away from his wife. At one point in 1989, he even threatened her with physical violence if she kept calling the house. But Dana continued to call her sister regularly. She was extremely worried about both Lisa and her child.

By August of 1990, Jack was gone most of the time, returning to Memphis only on weekends. At that point, Lisa decided to leave Jack. With Dana's help, she began to look for her own apartment. They found a place and began plans to move out. However, Jack found out about the plans and became furious. He called Lisa from a job he was working in Idaho, pleading with her not to leave and threatening her. The message was recorded on the home phone recorder. A similar message was left with Union Planters where Lisa was employed. On August 27, against her sister's advice, Lisa agreed to meet with Jack and planned to tell him that she was leaving the marriage. Lisa took her child to a babysitter, and Jack picked her up at 11:00 p.m. She died in a car accident later that night. In the investigation that followed Lisa's death, Jack was found to have alcohol, Ecstasy, and cocaine in his bloodstream. He was charged with vehicular homicide and reckless driving. There was no trial, and Jack spent three months in prison after agreeing to a plea bargain.

During my kidnapping, Jordan told me of the tragedy that befell him on August 27, 1990. He told me that on that night he lost his only real love, and that his life went downhill from then on due to sorrow, alcohol, and incarceration. I felt sympathetic toward him. He said that he developed a drug problem in prison, but there were not adequate programs to help him. He attended church services and AA, but he did not overcome his addictions. He claimed that he also studied for a bachelor's degree in sociology and acquired 111 hours of credits, but he did not end up qualifying for the degree. When he got out of jail, Jordan turned to crime to support his drug addiction. He committed a string of serious felonies and served a ten-year sentence in prison from 1994 to 2004.

State of Texas v. Jack Lindsey Jordan

DISTRICT ATTORNEY BLOUNT: In 1994, when you were thirty-one years old, you committed four felony offenses for which you pled guilty in Tarrant County. True?

JORDAN: Yes sir.

BLOUNT: One of those was theft of a vehicle.

JORDAN: Yes.

BLOUNT: There was a separate burglary of habitation.

JORDAN: Yes sir.

BLOUNT: There was a robbery causing bodily injury.

JORDAN: Yes sir.

BLOUNT: Is it true that in the city of Bedford on February 20 of 1994 that you entered someone's home through the garage door and took a purse from the kitchen and a camera and jewelry from the bedroom?

JORDAN: I did enter that habitation through the garage.

BLOUNT: And went into the house, didn't you?

JORDAN: Yes sir, I did.

BLOUNT: On another burglary that you pled guilty to in 1994 you entered into a homeowner's garage and stole a vehicle. Is that true?

JORDAN: Yes sir.

BLOUNT: A robbery involved your attempt to steal money from a female, true?

JORDAN: Yes sir.

BLOUNT: And that occurred right around the time of the other burglaries?

JORDAN: Same day.

BLOUNT: Did you go to a mall?

JORDAN: Yes, I was at a mall.

BLOUNT: You saw a female?

JORDAN: Yes sir.

BLOUNT: You went up behind her and jumped on her back?

JORDAN: No sir.

BLOUNT: Grabbed her around the neck?

JORDAN: No sir.

BLOUNT: Almost knocked her to the ground?

JORDAN: It says . . .

BLOUNT: No, did you or did you not?

JORDAN: I did not.

BLOUNT: Did you grab her purse?

JORDAN: Yes, I did.

BLOUNT: Did you pull it from her?

JORDAN: Yes, I did.

BLOUNT: Did you hurt her?

JORDAN: I don't know. I hope I didn't.

BLOUNT: Well, when you grab someone's purse and pull it from them against their will . . . You tell us that you didn't intend to hurt that person and if it did happen you just didn't mean for it to happen?

JORDAN: That is correct.

BLOUNT: Mr. Jordan, you commit these crimes and then you hope it works out for the best. Haven't you made the statement before that you are the nicest most nonviolent robber in the state of Texas?

JORDAN: When I'm not on methamphetamines, I am a good person.

BLOUNT: Well, you walked into Dr. Berk's home through an open garage door hoping that no one was home, right?

JORDAN: Yes sir.

BLOUNT: So you hoped it would turn out right?

JORDAN: Yes sir.

BLOUNT: It is fact though that when you did go in through the garage door there were two vehicles parked in the garage? Right?

JORDAN: Yes sir.

BLOUNT: And you hoped that no one was home?

JORDAN: Yes sir.

BLOUNT: You pulled into their garage and got out and went into the house?

JORDAN: Yes sir.

BLOUNT: So you were just taking the chance that no one was at home?

JORDAN: Yes sir.

BLOUNT: Now when you entered the home you heard some sound.

JORDAN: Yes sir, I heard a TV.

BLOUNT: Which would indicate that someone was home?

JORDAN: Not necessarily, but maybe.

BLOUNT: Did it occur to you that someone might be home and it would be a good idea to leave at that point?

JORDAN: Yes, I did.

BLOUNT: Then why didn't you leave?

JORDAN: I made a really bad choice.

In May 2004, Jordan was released on parole. He originally stayed with his mother, but in February 2005, after many warnings, she told him that he could not stay in her house any longer. He changed his address without notifying his parole officer and committed a robbery. These were the "technicalities" Jordan was referring to when he told me that his parole violation and my kidnapping were the result of mistakes. An arrest warrant was issued for Jordan in Lubbock on March 1. His crime spree began on March 2. He had no place to go, and he was addicted to methamphetamines. He told me and others that he would never go back to prison, that he would never be taken alive.

After my kidnapping, details about Jordan's crime spree hit all the local networks. Lubbock's Fox 34 News reported that on March 2, a woman in Terry County returned home to find a white SUV in her driveway. As the woman entered her house, a man armed with a gun opened the door from the inside. He told her to come in and then robbed her of cash and weapons.

Lubbock's NewsChannel 11 reported on the second crime. On Saturday, March 5, Jordan came to the home of a man whom he had just been introduced to by a mutual friend. The man, who wished to remain anonymous, asked Jordan to leave his home but Jordan refused. The victim told the reporter that Jordan had a gun and that they had started fighting. "Jordan was first beating the man on the head with his fists and then started using a piece of metal. The victim believed that Jordan wanted him dead."

The victim was quoted as saying, "Once I had my hand on the gun I didn't think about that anymore. It was just, 'How many times is he going to hit me before he realizes he is not going to hurt me?' Then when he took the metal it started to hurt me but even that pain went away." TV footage showed that the man had a broken finger, a broken arm, and dozens of stitches on his face from the fight.[7]

Presumably, Jordan left Lubbock some time on Saturday and headed toward Amarillo via Interstate 27. He drove up Bell Street and into my subdivision. My garage door was open. I was un-lucky.

16

The Capture

After he left me in Bushland, Jack headed out Interstate 40 toward New Mexico. Perhaps he assumed that his intimidation tactics had worked, that the understanding doctor would stay silent about the morning's events. But it still made sense to put as much distance between himself and his crime as possible. I imagine that the adrenaline rush of committing a crime combined with his paranoia, and Jack sped down the highway at top speed. He had a full tank of gas, cash and several stolen credit cards, and a drawerful of jewelry that could be sold for cash or drugs. I imagine that he hardly noticed the landmarks he was speeding by: miles of prairie land, several giant natural lakes, and the town of Tucumcari on the banks of the Canadian River, just past the Texas–New Mexico border. He had no time for sightseeing or bird-watching, no interest in visiting the Mesalands Dinosaur Museum. He probably did not know that he passed the Mesa Redonda, a huge, multicolored, flat-topped hill that looks like a lunar projection. The infamous train robber

Black Jack Ketchum used the mesa as a hideout before he was caught, tried quickly, West Texas style, and sentenced to death. Jack Jordan would not have slowed down for these landmarks, but continued onward past Santa Rosa, a town with such deep lakes that scuba divers can receive their certification utilizing the eighty-foot-deep artesian well located downtown.

Jack's chosen destination was Albuquerque, New Mexico, about an hour from Santa Rosa. For Amarilloans and other tourists, Albuquerque is a quaint town of Indian arts and crafts, Mexican restaurants, the Old Town Plaza, anthropology museums, and an autumn hot air balloon festival. It is also the home of the University of New Mexico, college basketball games, Internet cafés, and a varied nightlife. But to Jack, Albuquerque is something quite different. It is a haven for street gangs and independent drug dealers peddling methamphetamines and crack cocaine. Seven percent of New Mexico high school students report the use of meth. And among U.S. high school students, those in New Mexico rank third for the highest prevalence of methamphetamine use. Many of the adult males and adolescents arrested in Albuquerque test positive for methamphetamines. Methamphetamine was detected in 22 percent of Albuquerque forensic lab tests.[18]

Almost immediately upon driving into town, Jack found an accomplice. He joined up with Danella Van Damme, also known as Vandella Williams, a twenty-five-year-old white female with long black stringy hair, a fair complexion, and large, sad eyes. Little is known about her either before or after Jack Jordan's crime spree, but she met up with Jack in Albuquerque and they sought to score drugs together. Shortly after arriving in Albuquerque, Jack loaned his white Montero to a man named Niño (who had no last name) to make a drug transaction. Jack unloaded Shirley's ring collection in exchange for drugs. That was the last Jack saw of Niño, the Montero, or the stolen property. Jack left Albuquerque with Danella in a red and white pickup truck, which apparently belonged to Van Damme's brother. Later, the white Montero was found in downtown Albuquerque. It contained rifle and shotgun ammunition, spent shells, and a prescription for a pain medication that had Jack Lindsey Jordan's name on it. Shirley's rings were lost forever.

It is unclear what Jack and Danella did on March 7, the day after my kidnapping. However, at midnight on March 8, they experienced car trouble as they headed west on Interstate 40 toward Arizona. At a truck stop just west of Gallup, New Mexico, they found themselves in the vulnerable position of running from the law with a truck that was so overheated it would have to be abandoned. They had to find another vehicle.

The Vannovers were tourists from Canada who were traveling across the American Southwest. They pulled up to the truck stop in their RV towing a white Grand Cherokee. Jack and Danella watched Mrs. Vannover as she headed to the restroom in the darkness. Jack crossed the parking lot and entered the cab of the RV through the passenger side door. He aimed his shotgun at Robert Vannover, who sat stunned, immobile, and frightened while Danella moved their belongings into the couple's Grand Cherokee. When Mrs. Vannover returned, she found her husband sitting pale and sweating in the driver's seat, shotgun at his back. Jack directed her to get in the car and then forced Mr. Vannover to drive to an isolated area in the desert. Danella followed behind in their overheated, but still functional, truck. During the terrifying ride, Mrs. Vannover was scared but also incredibly angry. She told Jack how ashamed he should be about his behavior.

The Vannovers, frightened, confused, and angry, were kidnapped in their own vehicle and moved to the desert. In an isolated location in the middle of the night, Jack told them to exit the vehicle. As they stepped out of the RV, I imagine they feared for their lives and contemplated being executed in the darkness, surrounded by great natural beauty. They both must have been heavy hearted to see a beloved spouse go from enjoying a vacation to trembling and contemplating death. The psychological trauma must have been unbearable for both of them.

However, Jack was not a murderer. He did not shoot them, but once again resorted to threats of revenge to discourage his victims from reporting his crimes. After terrorizing the Vannovers in the middle of the Arizona desert, Jack unhitched the Grand Cherokee and threw the keys to the RV into the darkened landscape. He and Danella were soon back on Interstate 40.

On the morning of March 9, while the Vannovers were recovering from shock and trauma and Jack and Danella were continuing their escape west, I was in Amarillo, explaining to the Texas Tech business office that they could not cancel my stolen Tech credit card. The Texas Rangers were using it to track Jack's progress across the country. Jack's family told the rangers that they did not know where he was, and they warned that he would not likely be captured alive. On March 9, in Flagstaff, Arizona, Jack and Danella spent $6.15 on food at a KFC. They filled their new Grand Cherokee with gas and spent several hundred dollars at Walmart.

Detective Bill Fancher of the Kingman, Arizona, police force had been working with Amarillo police and Texas rangers. He was expecting Jack to pass through Kingman, which was the next major exit along Interstate 40. Detective Fancher was aware that Jack was wanted for kidnapping and that he was driving a stolen white Grand Cherokee. As luck would have it, a vehicle matching the description given by the Vannovers passed through a down-town Kingman park as Detective Fancher was doing paperwork. Realizing that this could be the wanted criminal, the detective turned on his lights and sirens and began to pursue the vehicle. Jack sped recklessly through the wide main streets of Kingman, going through stop signs and stoplights and endangering the public safety. Members of the Arizona Department of Public Safety and Kingman Police Department were radioed for assistance. Jack, with Danella brandishing a rifle out the window, found his way back to Interstate 40 traveling at speeds well above ninety miles per hour.

Stop sticks placed by the Department of Public Safety successfully exploded Jack's tires at a roadblock set up on I-40 outside of Kingman. With sparks flying, he continued to drive on the bare rims. He pulled off at a Kingman westbound exit, drove off an embankment, and ran into a wire fence. The Grand Cherokee was totaled.

Danella remained in the car, but Jack, unable to admit the end, ran for the freedom he said he would never give up. He did not take his rifles or shotguns with him. He was pursued by eight officers. I imagine the scene with police sirens blaring, numerous flashing red lights, and the fluctuating hum of passing 18-wheelers. I imagine Jack's heavy breathing and grunts of pain as he made his last futile efforts for freedom.

Jack, now you are the frightened one, pursued by aggressive police officers and wondering if you will be shot down. Now the firearms are aimed at your back. I know you are cursing your bad luck, agonized by back pain as you run for your life, blaming others for your serious misfortunes. It is not the mistake in Memphis, but so many other mistakes that have brought you to this moment. I take no joy in this at all. In fact, it is with sorrow that I mourn your life, which is now bereft of all purpose.

Jack Lindsey Jordan ran through the wide-open Arizona desert, through its tangles of heavy brush and the occasional blue and yellow wildflowers. He ran, despite the pain, because it was the only scene left to be played out. He ran through the needle-sharp thorns of new-growth mesquite, the cat's-claw thorns of the acacias. He ran for his freedom, but there was no place to run to and no place to hide.

Within minutes he was overtaken by three policemen, who tackled and handcuffed him. They probably were not pleased with the high-speed chase, which had jeopardized the safety of Kingman citizens. Jack asked for water, complained of rough treatment, and asked to be taken to the nearest hospital. His outrageous criminal behavior had finally ended. He was taken alive.

Thomas Bauman, supervisor of the U.S. Marshalls service, speaking from Albuquerque, said that Jack's capture was "a very big victory for both law enforcement and the communities in all states affected. [Jordan] was on a continual criminal rampage and told associates he would not stop until police took him down" and that "the case was the biggest in the country right now."[19]

In Jack's vehicle were found the guns and rifles stolen from Leslie's home. My credit card was found in his wallet. Jack was taken to a local hospital complaining of chest pain but was not found to have heart disease. Strapped to a gurney and complaining of severe back pain, he confessed to my kidnapping. When asked about what type of firearm was used, he asked for an attorney.

Later that day, I received a call from Amarillo police informing me that Jack had been arrested. It had been three days, and I had not yet returned to work. It was time to put away my revolver and return to the regional dean's office. When asked for comment, I told the *Amarillo Globe-News* reporter, "Obviously I am relieved for myself and I have worried about the safety of others. I am glad that he will have to answer for his crimes, but I hope there might be the possibility of rehabilitation as well."[20]

17

The Trial

T he *State of Texas v. Jack Lindsey Jordan* trial began in February of 2007, almost two years after the crime took place. For me it was of little significance, as I had not been physically or emotionally harmed and had not felt any need for revenge or retribution. I had been told that Jordan might plead insanity or seek a different venue because of the high level of pretrial publicity, hence the delay. As a crime victim in Texas I was asked to give my opinion on the time in prison that would be reasonable as punishment to match the crime. I had found that determination difficult. However, when forty years was suggested, I thought that to be excessive.

I met with both the district attorney's office and the defense team just prior to the trial. At my initial meetings I did not really feel allegiance to one or the other but just tried to clarify some of the particulars of the case. I was asked by the prosecutor's office about the long-term emotional effects of my ordeal and affirmed that I had not been harmed, had not sought professional help, did not have post-traumatic stress syndrome, sleep problems, or nightmares. Because I wrote a statement at the time of the kidnapping, I was very, very clear on all aspects of the experience, with the exception of not knowing exactly where we had waited for a public telephone to use. While I did not know the difference between a rifle and a shotgun at the time of the kidnapping, I did come to learn the difference. The dedication and attention to detail of the district attorney's office was formidable. District Attorney Farren had put Cynthia Evans on the case, though at trial she would work in tandem with David Blount. Cindy Evans was young, pretty, petite, energetic, and very professional. If she had been a physician, I would have wanted her on my team. David Blount was a very experienced attorney, tall, understated, and professorial, who knew West Texas and its people. Ms. Evans had great respect for me as a person and as a physician. I always believed that she thought that I had done the right things, that I had made successful choices that had protected me and my family.

The defense first sent a private investigator to talk with me, and later I was visited by Defense Attorney Bailey. I agreed to have my testimony taped by the defense, as I felt there was only one truth to this story and I had every intention of telling that truth. I had no obligation to even meet with the defense team. I liked Mr. Bailey on our first meeting. He was about my age, short and stocky, with a constant smile and good sense of humor. He looked out of place in his shirt and tie, and I thought that he had likely risen from high school class clown to go on to law school for all the right reasons. He was a public defender, and I admired him for that. He was trying to represent Mr. Jordan in the most effective way possible.

Mr. Bailey was most interested in the conversation that went on between me and Mr. Jordan. There was an amusing side to the constant chatter between the kidnapper and the doctor. He obviously thought the personal side of things would mitigate the perception of his client as dangerous or deranged, and in some part I would agree. More importantly, Mr. Jordan's story of the death of his wife expressed with very genuine emotion, and the fact that his wife's death did seem to mark the beginning of a downhill course, was thought to be helpful to the case. Mr. Bailey also emphasized that where Jack had left me in Bushland was a safe place, very safe, and I had to agree. (The overall safety of the place that a kidnapping victim is left is one consideration at the time of sentencing.) Mr. Bailey, upon leaving our meeting, made the comment that his client was stupid, very stupid, but perhaps not very dangerous. For a moment this affable public defender gave me pause to be concerned. I remember saying to him, "Mr. Bailey, at the trial, whatever happened, happened." And he repeated, "Yes, what happened, happened." But I would never have imagined the scenario that he would suggest as truth at the trial, that Mr. Jordan entered my home but left his shotgun in his car. This comical, happy-go-lucky defender did change my opinion of public defenders forever. Yes, when it was all over we did shake hands, and I did say, "I know you were just doing your job," but really I was overly generous.

Between the time of the crime and the trial, I had moved to Lubbock, Texas, where I became dean of the Texas Tech University Health Sciences Center School of Medicine, supervising campuses in Amarillo, El Paso, Permian Basin, and Lubbock. On the morning of the trial, Shirley and I drove from Amarillo to Bushland. I had been asked how far it was between where I was left off by Mr. Jordan and where I jogged to flag down a passerby. I thought I would measure it exactly. The brief trip also served as a reminder of the ordeal and put my subsequent celebration of life in better focus.

The trial of the State of Texas versus Jack Lindsey Jordan was one of the first to take place in the new Randall County Courthouse. The building was part of the rejuvenation of the downtown area, across the street from West Texas A&M, where I visited frequently on various collaborative efforts between Tech and WT. The building may be the most impressive in all of Canyon, light brick with a large facade of glass. Texas takes great pride in its courthouses. While this one did not have the historic accoutrements, it was modern and spacious.

For almost the entire trial, Shirley and I were secluded. We waited in a small room outside the district attorney's office. We did know that a few friends had come to the trial to provide moral support. We had brought my mom and a cousin, Louise, who was about to move from New York to Amarillo. My dad had died between the time of the crime and trial. In attendance were a few doctors from the medical school: Marjorie Jenkins, Stephanie Leeper, and Afzal Siddiqui, all who had come to Amarillo with me from East Tennessee. A very loyal patient, Marshall Fitzwater, was at the trial for the duration, including the late-night final verdict. But this trial was a very old story by now, and few of those who had been there for us in March of 2005 even knew the trial was occurring. Tellingly, no one was there for Jack Jordan. Not even his mother attended the trial.

After several hours I was brought to an anteroom right outside the courtroom, then brought to my chair to testify. As I took the oath and sat down, I could see the jury over to the right but did not maintain eye contact with them. The judge was over my shoulder to the left. Attorneys Cindy Evans and David Blount faced me at their desk. To my left were Mr. Bailey and the defendant Jack Lindsey Jordan.

Of course, I had seen Mr. Jordan only once in person, and that was over two years before. He appeared to have gained upper body weight, and looked more formidable than I remembered. His hair appeared darker, and his overall appearance was much more respectable. My mom would later say that he looked very distinguished and not capable of the crime. From across the room his glance was cold—definitely not a friendly reunion.

I was examined by Mr. Blount and cross-examined by Mr. Bailey. I told my story as I had told it so many times before; I had prepared by rereading the account I gave right after the crime was committed. Much of the proceedings of the trial and my testimony have been included in the text of the story that you have already read.

Mr. Blount questioned me so that the events of that day could be retold succinctly. Examination and cross-examination focused on my level of fear at various times during the kidnapping.

Mr. Bailey asked questions to shed doubt on the level of danger that I actually faced. On my return to the house, why did I not just close the door and call 911 or run out the front door to someplace of safety? My answer clearly was that the action would put both my wife and me in jeopardy—that this defiance would make Mr. Jordan angry and dangerous. But it is a legitimate question and a very legitimate alternative action as compared to getting back in the car. To Mr. Bailey, it meant that perhaps Mr. Jordan was not really very threatening to me.

Bailey asked if Jordan and I had a gentleman's agreement that he would not go in the house. In court, I chose to say that this was not a true gentleman's agreement since Jordan had a gun. But Bailey said, "Isn't that the exact term you used when I visited you?" "Well, that may be," I replied.

Bailey wanted to make the point that with Jordan pumping gas and me in the car, there was a great opportunity to run, run through the open fields of Bushland. I told him that I feared being shot. And Bailey wanted to know about the fist bump on leaving the car. Who actually initiated it? To him my initiating this modern handshake, again, might suggest that the whole encounter was not being seen by me as dangerous. He asked if I had hugged Jordan on leaving his vehicle. I was surprised by this suggestion, but he said it was what I had told his investigator. (I had the opportunity to listen later to the taped recording with the investigator. There was no such comment.)

Bailey also surprised me with the question, "How could you not know exactly where you had gone that day and yet be able to memorize the vehicle registration number?" I said that memorizing the number was a matter of record. He asked, "What record?" I meant that I had given the number to the Amarillo police and that they had confirmed its accuracy.

The trial proceeded with Shirley's testimony, which was embarrassing for her, especially in cross-examination by the defense. She sees her husband pop into the kitchen, take her jewelry and wallet, and leave, saying only "Don't ask." She says she thought I might be going to a flea market to buy her a ring. Ridiculous! But should she have thought instead that I was being kidnapped and had a minute to get back to my kidnapper's car?

There was testimony from the Lubbock, Amarillo, Albuquerque, and Kingman police departments, the FBI, and the Texas Rangers. The evidence against Jordan was overwhelming, not only for my kidnapping but for other crimes during his rampage just after violating parole. The district attorney's office carefully provided details that all painted a very incriminating picture of guilt and of a desperate man addicted to methamphetamines who had violated parole just after serving ten years in prison. Evidence included my photo identification of Jordan, the vehicle registration number, my credit card in his wallet on his capture, his confession in Arizona, the identification of the guns he stole at the home of Leslie, and her identification of his SUV based on the missing "N."

The jury determined Jordan's guilt over lunch unanimously without controversy.

The punishment phase of the trial had Jordan deciding to testify, against the advice of his attorney, Mr. Bailey. His testimony laid him open for cross-examination about every crime he had ever committed, particularly the robbery of Leslie.

With respect to my kidnapping, he agreed with my testimony minus one issue. He claimed that he did not bring his shotgun into my house but that it was in his car. Mr. Bailey, stuck with the evidence at hand, chose to paint the same scenario, saying in his closing that "Dr. Berk says he pulled a gun on him, Jack says he did not." And so my caveat to him that "what happened, happened" was violated.

The district attorney painted Jordan as a dangerous criminal, much more dangerous than I would have ever imagined on the day of my kidnapping. As demonstrated by the prosecution, Jordan was capable of violence, as in the example of Whit, who was beaten up so badly that an orbital fracture resulted and twenty stitches were required to the face. Furthermore, Jordan could be very cruel, such as when he encountered the Canadian couple in the New Mexico desert, stole their Grand Cherokee, and threw away the keys to their RV. I am sure that the jury was most affected, however, by the story of the robbery of Leslie in Meadow because of the psychological damage that it had caused her—a grandmother afraid to have her own children and grandchildren visit her in her own home. Jordan had no respect for individual rights, as he demonstrated with my kidnapping. During the trial, he lied frequently and outrageously, and had absolutely no remorse.

Yet, I had seen the good in that individual, the good that lies in all of us, and I took no pleasure in the events of the trial.

Mr. Blount stated to the jury in his closing, "You have the power to see that these things never happen again. And that is by giving him a life sentence."

The result was quick and predictable.

"We the jury find Mr. Jordan guilty of the offense of aggravated kidnapping. And we assess his punishment and confinement in the Texas Department of Criminal Justice for life."

Leslie and I previously had never spoken or met, but we shared a common experience with a dangerous criminal. She had been traumatized two years earlier and she now found justice. While Jack Lindsey Jordan was not on trial for her case, only mine, his decision to testify at the sentencing hearing opened him up to be cross-examined on any previous crime. While I had no interest in the opportunity for the victim to confront his assailant, she asked me to speak for both of us, and I did not want to refuse. Leslie is a special person and a most unfortunate victim. And on that day I could see her healing, sensed her courage, and was inspired by her appreciation for the blessing of justice.

"Mr. Jordan, I was a victim of your crime, and you could have apologized to me today and taken responsibility for your action. Instead you decided to further try to hurt me with your absurd statement that you did not remember having a shotgun during the kidnapping and your trivializing the true events. Leslie and I could have profited from your apology as we hope for peace in your repentance. I had not met Leslie before today, and surely you realize that your repeatedly menacing manner with a gun, your particularly intimidating way of threatening the murder of family members, and your chilling warnings about not calling the police which you imposed on both of us validated our stories despite your continued denials. Someday I hope you admit to your crimes and ask forgiveness."

Shirley and I and Leslie and Lloyd promised ourselves that we would someday get together for a Tech football game. While that never happened, I do often hope for her full recovery. My animosity toward Jordan comes more from her experience than my own.

Amarillo Globe-News

Life in prison. That's the sentence a Randall County jury delivered to Jack Lindsey Jordan.

The jury found Jordan, 43, guilty in the kidnapping of Dr. Steven Berk from his Puckett home on March 6, 2005, and determined the sentence late Thursday.

At the time of the kidnapping, Berk was regional dean of the Texas Tech Health Science Center School of Medicine in Amarillo. Berk became Texas Tech University's new dean of the Health Science Center School of Medicine in Lubbock in March 2006.

After the kidnapping, Jordan forced Berk to drive him around for about two hours and tried to get Berk to get him money and drugs.

Russ Bailey, defense attorney for Jordan said his client was unhappy with the outcome of the trial.

"I'm not amazed about what the jury came back with, but I was hoping for better," Bailey said. "The jury did its job properly, the state did its job and I did my job. They ruled on the evidence that came in."[21]

James Farren, Randall County district attorney, said Jordan received two life sentences, one for each count. Those counts were aggravated robbery and aggravated kidnapping.

"We're grateful that the jury has taken a very dangerous man off the street. Randall County is not a good place to be found guilty."[22]

18

The Dream

After the trial, we drove back from Amarillo to Lubbock in darkness. The trial had been emotionally draining. Meeting the victims of Jordan's crime spree and hearing his testimony gave me a better appreciation of the danger that I faced on the day of the kidnapping. At home, the need for sleep overwhelmed a desire to ponder the day's events. As consciousness slipped away, my last thoughts were about how different the outcome of March 6, 2005, could have been.

I am sitting in the passenger seat of a white SUV, staring at the bright silver handle, which glints like the steel ring of a childhood merry-go-round. It looks so inviting, but I do not have the courage to grasp it. We are traveling at very high speed, and I feel like my time for brash action is running out. It is now or never. I push the door handle down and hurtle out of the speeding car, feeling myself slipping, falling, losing my breath, and tumbling without control, faster than the laws of physics should allow. My body is thrown through the tall yucca plants and into a barbed-wire fence lining the road. I land faceup in the dirt. The sun is directly overhead, and weeds and wildflowers obscure my view. I could lie here and hope for mercy from the driver of the SUV, who has surely stopped to reclaim his captive. But I am overwhelmed by the impulse to run. I am on my feet in an instant. My legs churn as if they are on a high-endurance treadmill, though I feel like I am going nowhere. I try to scream but cannot make a sound. The sound of a shotgun blast echoes across the meadow. I feel the burning pain across the back of my head, my shoulders, and legs. I finally understand the difference between a shotgun and a rifle. It is not a single bullet, but a spray of stinging pellets that tear through my skin and destroy all the tissues that lie beneath. I am on my back again. Shortly, the searing pain subsides, and I struggle to stay awake as the sky turns dark blue. I crawl to a nearby farmhouse, but as I arrive, the farmhouse transforms to a more familiar medical school building.

A crowd has gathered in the Women's Health and Research building, in the largest auditorium on the Texas Tech University Health Sciences Center campus. There is a large elevated stage with flags of the United States, Texas, and Texas Tech. There is a closed simple wooden casket at the base of the stage.

The eyes of familiar faces look right through me. I hear whispers from around the room and slowly realize what has happened. My body was found in a ditch by a farmer somewhere between Amarillo and Bushland. I suffered multiple trauma from shotgun blasts to the head and back. I had been missing for four weeks, and there was no explanation for my disappearance. The only things missing were the clothes I was wearing that Sunday morning, my wallet, and the garage door opener. A search in

Amarillo had turned up nothing. Then my body was finally found and the questions answered.

The death was related to a crime spree that extended from Lubbock to Meadow and into New Mexico all at about the same time—that one week in March. A criminal had invaded a family home and stolen the shotguns from the gun cabinet after terrorizing the lady of the house. A Lubbock man had been put into the hospital with facial fractures caused by the butt of a shotgun. It was thought I was probably just another victim of this violent criminal.

The auditorium fills with white coats—students, residents, and faculty—physicians all. My own voice fills the hall. It is a speech I gave to the first-year medical students when they received the symbol of their new profession.

> Your white coats mean that you have been invited into a prestigious profession. One where you will be a trusted and intimate participant in life's greatest and most elemental moments: birth, survival, miraculous cure, rehabilitation, but also sorrow, pain, and death. Few are able to go where we go. Priests and artists may see what we see, but they do not have the scientific gift that we are given, the gift to change lives, cure disease, and end suffering. Wherever you go, you will be exalted, respected, and very well paid. But there will be responsibility, awesome responsibility that comes with the most noble of professions. Those responsibilities you must accept in your oath. To hold sacred the physician-patient relationship protecting privacy and autonomy. To be honest with patients about options and about mistakes, for we will all make them. And to care for all patients, especially

the most vulnerable. To respect and understand cultural diversity and human frailty. To commit to the lifelong pursuit of learning and scientific inquiry. To keep the capacity for compassion with every patient no matter how difficult.

The room fills with colleagues and friends, fewer than I would have expected, but there are spring thunderstorms in the Panhandle. Among the white coats, one is different—a chef's jacket. Eric, my patient who was on the brink of death from HIV disease, is alive and accompanied by his teenage daughter.

Dr. McGovern, a former Catholic priest and professor of ethics, stands behind a podium. In his seventies, he still has a full head of the whitest hair, rosy cheeks, and a constant smile. He speaks with an Irish brogue. His eyes fill with tears as they have done at all the funerals I have seen him direct. He talks about my life and my career. I am glad he does not say that God needed me to teach students or treat pneumonia or raise money for the March of Dimes in heaven. I am glad he does not say that this was preordained. No, the garage door was left open and I was a victim of circumstance. No other explanation is necessary.

Dr. McGovern understands that a physician's work is not about published papers or books, honors or awards, titles or position. He knows that our greatest legacy lies in mentoring, inspiring, and strengthening others. Clifton, a former student from Johnson City, comes to the podium. He looks like he could be a professional football player, but he wears the white coat of a doctor. He says he would never have made it through medical school if not for me. A close friend, now a dean, comes forward and remembers when I stood for him against a very powerful CEO in East Tennessee, putting my own career in jeopardy. Others speak whose careers I helped to preserve.

There is a golden balcony section jutting out high above the auditorium that I had not noticed before. I climb the spiral steps to the balcony and see familiar faces at the top of the spiral staircase, young and old. I greet them as if I am head of a receiving line. They all have one thing in common: absolute aequanimitas; and so do I.

Two teenagers run from their seats toward me. Their bodies are young, strong, and whole. "Mr. Steve," says Kevin. "Still our very favorite counselor. But you gave up on finding the cure for muscular dystrophy awfully quickly."

"Good thing you won't be judged on that alone," his friend Pat says with a smile. "Well, you did discover the best way to get handicapped campers to catch fish."

"And speaking of judgment," says Mr. Montaigne, peering through thick glasses and still with his hair perfectly parted. "I wouldn't have expected you to miss such a serious drug interaction problem." I recognize his kindly smile, which now has a complete set of healthy white teeth.

"Had there been time, I would have liked to explain my mistake, to apologize."

"All of us have made mistakes, but we leave our regrets behind when we get here. Yours and those of your profession just tend to be more problematic. Turned out there was a weakened artery in my brain—that part wasn't your fault. But you doctors sure can make some big-time mistakes."

"I always tried to learn from mine."

"And you did. Do you know that in Memphis about ten years after my death, a patient with a heart infection also got placed on rifampin and Coumadin, just like I did? One of your former students picked up on it and got the regimen changed. Saved that patient's life. He told his team that Dr. Berk always warned him about antibiotic-Coumadin interactions."

"How would you know about all that?" I ask.

"All is known, all is revealed," he says, smiling and flashing his perfect teeth. "You will soon learn that you've made many more mistakes than you could ever have realized. But you have also done more good than you might have expected."

A young man steps forward. He has a stocky build, brown skin with a round face and high cheekbones. His sleek black hair is pulled back in a short ponytail. He looks to be in his early thirties. He wears a Tuba City Warriors T-shirt and jeans with a large silver belt buckle.

"No, you won't recognize me," he says softly. "I've changed quite a bit from when you last saw me at age three. My name is Ed Begay. I'm told that you treated me for diphtheria, and that with the heart involvement and all, I wouldn't have made it without you."

"That was the only diphtheria case I ever saw. At Keams Canyon in 1975, I remember. But how is it that you're here now?"

"Nothing to do with diphtheria. It was a drunken driver on Route 264 to Tuba City. Sometimes you're just in the wrong place at the wrong time. But I had twenty-eight good years and a child on the way. Maybe he'll want to be a doctor."

A distinguished young man with brownish red hair and ruddy cheeks is seated with a group of young residents. His name is embroidered on his white coat: Dr. Tom Ronald, professor of medicine. He rises to meet me. His melanoma scar is gone.

"My team has many arrivals to see today, but we had to stop by. It's busy, lots to do, you know, patching up everyone who is sent up here, but you wouldn't believe all the new therapeutics available. You'll really be pleased. Sorry about your ordeal, but we'll see you on rounds."

I look down from the balcony to view the mourners, but a fog surrounds the first row: my wife, my mom and dad in their eighties, Justin and Jeremy. They are obscured. I cannot see their faces, cannot hear them. An impenetrable cloud hovers over them. Yes, I understand the front-row fog. And I ask, please protect them from any bitterness and long-standing sorrow. And there is a whisper. Yes, they will be protected. And so I have no regrets.

19

Purpose

On March 6, 2005, I was spared to see another day, a crime victim who gave thanks for life itself. My story is unique, but I feel like a brother or sister to many others—those who walked away from a demolished car, whose heart stopped and started again, who survived the loss of a breast or colon, who were born weighing a pound but came off a ventilator and lived. We do not understand how we as a group differ from the nonsurvivors: those who were killed by their kidnapper, died at the hands of a drunken driver, succumbed to a heart attack or breast cancer, or never came home from the hospital. For now, we are alive and they are not. We are no smarter, no more religious, no more favored. To believe otherwise is to dishonor the memory of those who have died tragically, violently, or prematurely. I love to think, as some have suggested, that an angel was hovering over me. However, that angel may have a more pressing assignment the next time.

I suspect that we who survive have some purpose. We serve as reminders that life is precious, unpredictable, and beyond our control. We need to protect our lives—in my case, to keep the garage door closed. For others it will mean exercising, stopping smoking, obtaining the yearly mammogram, or wearing a seat belt. But in the end, our fates are in God's hands, and our lives are on loan. None of us are guaranteed safety, health, or old age.

We are given a chance each day to see the beauty of life around us, to find a role for ourselves in making life better for someone, to express our appreciation for what time we do have. I promised myself, during my abduction, that I would scream for joy if I was released. I never really made that scream but have instead quietly and constantly screamed for the joy of my freedom.

To the community of Amarillo, which had been concerned about my ordeal, I wanted to say more than just "thank you" and more than just "keep your garage door closed." I wrote in the Amarillo paper, "If you have been leaving something undone— an act of kindness or forgiveness, finding your college roommate or lost friend, saying yes to that charity that you never had time for, or just getting back to that great place you remember fondly—the sun is likely shining today in Amarillo. It is your day, your gift, your time."[23]

It was a spring day in Lubbock, Texas, the evening of graduation for all medical students from Texas Tech School of Medicine. Faculty and students from the campuses of Lubbock, Amarillo, and El Paso met, along with their families, to celebrate the graduation of the Class of 2005.

As always, I had come to know almost all of the students personally and shared the intense pride of the students' families on that day. Medical school graduation is a momentous occasion and a time for celebration.

For me, this May 2005 graduation was special. I was still thanking people for their concern about my kidnapping and still answering questions about what happened. Prior to the kidnapping, I had been elected by the students of Amarillo to do their hooding ceremony. While I had not spent much time in the trenches with the students, I had taught them in small groups and imparted values about ethics, geriatrics, and the principles of infectious disease. I advised them on the residency match and career opportunities, and often called program directors to try to help them get into the program that was their first choice.

The students marched into the auditorium to "Pomp and Circumstance." I am always very moved by the music, the tradition, the caps and gowns of the faculty representing different schools from around the country. Most gowns are black, but the older medical schools have kept their distinct colors, so I wear the bright red gown of Boston University, the same gown I wore as a student. I was on stage, in the very bright lights with other deans, soon to step forward and perform the hooding ceremony for my students.

I had done the hooding ceremony a dozen times before, but that night was different. My usual sweaty palms, hand wringing, and unsteady legs were completely gone. I hooded each student and shook their hand. In fact, I shook their hand twice—once before the hood was placed and again just after the hooding was performed. I had learned to enjoy the moment. In a way, I too had graduated.

Jack Lindsey Jordan taught me a lesson using his temper, his shotgun, his attempt at intimidation. I could not afford to fret over small things or imagined fears again. I would celebrate my life, my experiences, and my contributions at every opportunity. I would fear no evil, large or small. I had come much closer to a life of aequanimitas.

Perhaps that is the most important lesson coming from my experience: to live each day to its fullest; to celebrate the joys of family, work, and good health; and to appreciate our every moment as precious.

Notes

1. William Osler, *Aequanimitas* (New York: Blakiston Company, 1904), 3–11.
2. Jerry L. Spivack, "Polycythemia Vera and Other Myeloproliferative Diseases," in *Harrison's Principles of Internal Medicine,* ed. Anthony S. Fauci et al. (New York: McGraw-Hill, 2008), 671–74.
3. George Schwarz, "After Beating Odds, Tech Dean Relives Ordeal," *Amarillo Globe-News,* March 8, 2005, 5A.
4. Texas Performance Review, "Reduce Recidivism of Adults Leaving the Texas Correctional System," http://www.window.state.tx.us/tpr/tpr4/c3.psc/c301.html (accessed June 12, 2005).
5. Ibid.
6. National Institute on Drug Abuse, "Methamphetamine Abuse and Addiction," http://www.nida.nih.gov/researchreports/methamph/mcthamph.html (accessed October 25, 2010).
7. Ibid.
8. Joan E. Zweben, Judith B. Cohen, Darrell Christian, Gantt P. Galloway, Michelle Salinardi, David Parent, and Martin Iguchi, for the Methamphetamine Treatment Project, "Psychiatric Symptoms in Methamphetamine Users," *American Journal on Addiction* 13 (2004): 181–90.
9. Ibid.

10. Victims Services Division, Crime Victim's Rights, Texas Department of Criminal Justice, http://www.tdcj.state.tx.us/victim/victim-billrights.htm (accessed October 24, 2010).

11. Enriques Rangel, "Home Intruders Are Being Shot to Death in Texas," *Lubbock Avalanche-Journal*, September 13, 2008.

12. Schwarz, "After Beating Odds, Tech Dean Relives Ordeal," 1.

13. Ibid., 5A.

14. Kris Abbey, "Alleged Kidnapper Psycho," *Amarillo Globe-News*, March 11, 2006, 1.

15. Ibid.

16. P. Christine Smith, "Robbery, Kidnapping Victim Puts Police on Suspect's Trail," *Lubbock Avalanche-Journal*, March 8, 2005, 1.

17. "Three State Manhunt Ends with a Man in Jail," http://www.kcbd.com/Global/story.asp?S=3056191&nav=CcXHXJF4 (accessed March 11, 2005).

18. Nina Shah, "Drug Abuse Patterns and Trends in Albuquerque and New Mexico," in *Epidemiologic Trends in Drug Abuse: Proceedings of the Community Epidemiology Work Group*, National Institute of Drug Abuse, vol. 2, June 2008, 1–10.

19. P. Christine Smith, "Kidnapping Suspect's Run Hits End," Lubbock Online.com, March 10, 2005, http://lubbockonline.com/stories/031005/loc_497735.shtml (accessed December 11, 2009).

20. Kris Abbey, "Local Kidnapping Suspect Captured in Arizona," *Amarillo Globe-News*, March 10, 2005, 1.

21. Josh Burton, "Jordan Gets Life in Prison," *Amarillo Globe-News*, February 10, 2007, http://amarillo.com/stories/2007/02/10/new_6769198.shtml (accessed December 31, 2010).

22. Ibid.

23. Steven Berk, M.D., "Purpose Provides Reason to Survive," *Amarillo Globe-News*, March 27, 2005, 5A.

DOGWATCHING

Desmond Morris

JONATHAN CAPE
THIRTY-TWO BEDFORD SQUARE LONDON

Line drawings by Edward Coleridge

First published 1986
Reprinted 1986
Text copyright © 1986 by Desmond Morris
Illustrations copyright © 1986 by Jonathan Cape Ltd

Jonathan Cape Ltd, 32 Bedford Square, London WC1B 3EL

British Library Cataloguing in Publication Data

Morris, Desmond
Dogwatching.
1. Dogs – Behaviour
I. Title
636.7   SF433

ISBN 0-224-02867-7

Typeset by Computape (Pickering) Ltd, North Yorkshire
Printed in Great Britain by
The Alden Press Ltd, Oxford

Contents

Introduction

In the whole of human history only two kinds of animals have been allowed the freedom of our homes: the cat and the dog. It is true that in earlier times farm animals were often brought into the home at night for security, but they were always penned or tethered. It is also true that in more recent times a wide variety of pet species have been kept inside our houses – fish in tanks, birds in cages, reptiles in vivaria – but all of these have been captives, separated from us by glass or wire or bars. Only cats and dogs have been permitted to wander from room to room and to come and go almost as they please. With them we have a special relationship, an ancient contract with quite specific terms of agreement.

Sadly, these terms have often been broken, and nearly always by us. It is a sobering thought that cats and dogs are more loyal, trustworthy and reliable than human beings. Very occasionally they turn on us, scratch us or bite us, or run away and leave us, but when this happens there is usually a piece of human stupidity or cruelty lurking in the background to provide a cause. For most of the time they unswervingly fulfil their half of the age-old bargain we have struck with them, and shame us by their conduct.

The contract that was drawn up between man and dog is over 10,000 years old. Had it been written down, it would have stated that if the dog performs certain tasks for us, we in return will provide it with food and water, and with shelter, companionship and care. The tasks it has been asked to carry out have been many and varied. Dogs have been required to guard our homes, protect our persons, aid our hunts, destroy our vermin, and pull our sledges. In more specialized roles, they have been trained to collect birds' eggs in their mouths without breaking the shells, locate truffles, sniff out drugs at airports, guide the blind, rescue avalanche victims, track down escaped criminals, run races, travel in space, act in films and compete as show dogs.

I

Occasionally the faithful dog has been unwittingly reduced to a human level of barbaric conduct. Today we think of the 'dogs of war' as human mercenaries – men who enjoy the macho thrill of maiming and killing with special weapons. But originally they were real dogs, trained to attack the front lines of an enemy army. Shakespeare is referring to this when he makes Mark Antony call out, 'Cry "Havoc!" and let slip the dogs of war'. The ancient Gauls retaliated by sending in armoured dogs, equipped with heavy collars bristling with razor-sharp knives. These terrifying animals, rushing and leaping at the Roman cavalry, tore the legs of their horses to shreds.

Regrettably, fighting dogs are still with us today. Although officially outlawed, pit fights between specially trained animals remain an excuse for gambling and for the savage entertainment of the more bloodthirsty elements of society. These contests have been forced to go underground but they have by no means been eliminated.

In some Eastern countries dogs are considered a food delicacy, but this has never been one of their major roles, and is steadily becoming less common. It appears to have been most widespread in China, where the name of the edible dog was the same as the slang word for food: chow. In most regions, however, dogs escaped the pot because they had so many other, more important uses.

One of the unfortunate side-effects of the great popularity of dogs in all human societies was the growth of the stray dog population. In some countries this canine surplus established itself as a disease-ridden scavenging horde that gave all dogs a bad name. The Pariah Dogs of the Middle East, in particular, turned human friendship into revulsion. In the doctrines of several religions the dog became 'unclean'. Over the years the very word became a term of contempt: dirty dog, filthy cur, pig-dog and dogsbody. Even today, in some ethnic groups, children learn the ancient tradition of despising the dog. The strongest survival of this attitude is found in Muslim cultures. Re-education in schools has proved an uphill struggle.

In the West a happier development has occurred. As the earlier tasks set for the dog have faded in importance, a new role has emerged. The working dog has been largely replaced